# That Good Night

A play

# N. J. Crisp

## Samuel French — London
New York - Toronto - Hollywood

© 1999 BY N. J. CRISP

## THAT GOOD NIGHT

First presented on 2nd April, 1996 by Marc Sinden for Smallhythe Productions Ltd in association with the Yvonne Arnaud Theatre, Guildford, with the following cast of characters:

| | |
|---|---|
| **Anna** | Lucy Fleming |
| **Michael** | Patrick Ryecart |
| **Debbie** | Julie-Kate Olivier |
| **Ralph** | Donald Sinden |
| **The Visitor** | Nigel Davenport |

Directed by Edward Hall
Designed by Michael Pavelka
Lighting designed by Robert Bryan

# CHARACTERS

**Anna**
**Michael**
**Debbie**
**Ralph**
**The Visitor**

The action takes place the courtyard/patio of a house in the Umbrian Hills, Italy

Time—the present

Other plays by N. J. Crisp published by Samuel French Ltd

Dangerous Obsession
Fighting Chance
Suspicions

# ACT I

## SCENE 1

*A courtyard/patio in the Umbrian Hills, Italy. An afternoon in midsummer*

*An attractive stone-flagged courtyard/patio occupies most of the stage. It is framed, as it were, by: 1. To the rear, facing us, an Italian house. It faces south, and, although the shutters are open, venetian blinds are down and closed in the windows, so that we cannot see inside. A door leads into the house, at present closed. We can only see part of the house, which either continues to the right and out of sight, or is L-shaped, the other part of the L running backwards and away from us. Behind the house, in the distance, are hills, shrouded in a purple haze. 2. L, a wall, up which climb appropriate clinging plants or shrubs, runs from the house to the front of the stage. It is tall enough that we cannot see over it. Entry is through an arched, wrought iron gate, standing open. Through the gate, a glimpse of more flagstones, and perhaps one or two flowering shrubs standing in carved stone pots. 3. R, shrubs and flowers complete the frame. There is a short path through them, and the presence of a swimming pool may be suggested*

*The courtyard itself is pleasantly set out with garden furniture, a table, an olive tree (or sun umbrella), a comfortable couch. Here and there are more potted plants. The effect of the whole is discreetly stylish, elegant, and thoroughly agreeable*

*Before the* CURTAIN *rises, music is coming from a portable radio near Anna*

*When the* CURTAIN *rises, Anna is sitting immersed in a book. She wears glasses, but only for reading. She is somewhere in her forties, with bare legs, sandals on her feet, her dress light and decorous. She is Austrian by birth, but her English has only the trace of an accent. Her manner is open and direct to the point sometimes of seeming innocence, although she possesses considerable shrewdness as well. She has the virtue of a fine simplicity without being naïve. Slim in build, her careless attractiveness is natural and without artifice. She can (as early on) carry on a bit in awkward social occasions*

*The sound of a car approaching from a distance, turning in, and coming to a stop brings her out of her book. She looks at her watch, as if disconcerted, takes off her glasses, lays them on the table, and switches off the radio*

*There is a murmur of a man's (Michael's) voice, off, low-pitched, speaking as if to a driver. Anna cannot make out the words*

**Michael** (*off, distant, murmuring*) You wait here. I'll make sure this is it.

*Michael comes into sight and moves through the gate. He is in his thirties, tall and well-built, casually dressed, his good looks interesting rather than handsome. A thoughtful man, a little reserved, with his share of introspections, it is perhaps his nice smile which shows a considerate good nature*

*Anna advances to meet him. They do not know each other well and, on Anna's side anyway, it shows*

**Anna** (*her smile pleasant*) Hallo. You managed to find us then. Was it difficult?
**Michael** (*an answering smile*) Easier than I thought. That's why I'm a bit early.

*They shake hands formally*

**Anna** Oh, but that's nice. We can have a chat first. Are you well? You look well. Hardly changed at all.
**Michael** (*drily*) Nor have you, Anna.
**Anna** (*unaware of his irony*) Did you come by taxi?
**Michael** No, I've rented a car.

*Anna moves away from him towards the chairs. Michael sort of hovers, still near the gate*

**Anna** I thought I heard you speaking to someone, that's all. Do come and sit down. (*She turns to face Michael*)
**Michael** I was talking to a friend of mine.
**Anna** Oh?
**Michael** You see, I had made other arrangements ...
**Anna** You've brought someone with you?
**Michael** If that's all right, yes.
**Anna** But of course. Do ask your friend to join us, please.

*Michael goes through the gate and out of sight. Again, there is the murmur of his voice*

**Michael** (*off, indistinguishable*) It is the right place. Come and meet Anna.

*There is the sound of a car door slamming, off*

*Michael comes through the gate, accompanied by Debbie. She is in her twenties. She is dressed for the heat, but very stylishly. She is also exceedingly glamorous*

Anna, this is Debbie.

*Anna advances to greet Debbie with a warm (genuine) smile*

**Anna** Ah, so this is your friend. A pleasure to meet you, Debbie.

*They shake hands politely*

**Debbie** Hallo, Anna.
**Anna** Do you like this weather?
**Debbie** Very much.
**Anna** So do I. It's raining in London. Did you know that?
**Debbie** No.
**Anna** It was on the radio. Well, let's make ourselves comfortable, shall we?

*They arrange themselves in chairs. In truth, it is all a little strained and awkward, but Anna sails on confidently*

Have you come from Rome?
**Michael** Yes.
**Anna** I shop there once a week, but really it's awful there this time of year, don't you think?
**Debbie** I like it.
**Anna** Do you really? So full of people. And the traffic. I prefer this. How do you like our little retreat?
**Debbie** It's beautiful.
**Anna** So are you. Although I expect you've been told that often enough.
**Debbie** Now and then.
**Anna** (*to Michael*) We won't disturb him. He works every afternoon, and hates to be interrupted.
**Michael** How is he?
**Anna** Oh, very well. The operation was a great success, you know.

**Michael** Good.

**Anna** He must take long walks, and I insist he swims in the pool at least once a day. Oh, yes, I make sure he does all the right things.

**Michael** (*wryly*) I'm sure you do, Anna.

**Anna** (*after a pause, looking at her watch*) He won't be long. It's nearly time.

**Michael** He must be doing a lot of thinking.

**Anna** Thinking? Yes, of course. He thinks all the time. What do you mean?

**Michael** Listen.

*Anna listens to the silence*

**Anna** I hear nothing.

**Michael** Exactly.

**Anna** Oh, you mean that noisy old typewriter he used to rattle away on.

**Michael** Yes.

**Anna** He finally got rid of that. Now, he uses one of those things with a screen.

**Michael** A PC. A word processor.

**Anna** That's it. Do you have one?

**Michael** Yes.

**Anna** I don't understand the thing. I'm terrified to touch it. And the sound of his typing. I miss that, somehow.

*During the following, the venetian blind at one of the windows is lifted. Ralph's face peers out. It is clear from his attitude that he has been lying down on a couch beside the window, and has lifted himself on one elbow to look out. Ralph is bleary eyed. He yawns, sinks back on to the couch and lets the venetian blind fall again*

**Michael** (*after another pause; they grow longer*) What's he working on?

**Anna** I don't know. He won't tell me. Will you ask him? He'd tell you, I'm sure.

**Michael** Yes, all right. If you like.

**Anna** I'd love to know. This will be his masterwork, oh, yes. Such intensity and concentration, so much hard work, it can be nothing less.

**Michael** Have you bought this place?

**Anna** Oh, no. Rented for the summer. It's perfect. Ideal, for his convalescence. Where could he take his long walks in London?

**Michael** Well, you're not far from Hyde Park. Or have you moved?

**Anna** (*firmly*) No, but this is better. Oh, he grumbled at first, but I had my own way in the end, and now he loves it. I'm sure we could pass the rest of our lives together here, and not miss London at all.

**Michael** Well, no reason why not. Perhaps you can persuade him to buy it.

**Anna** Perhaps. It has occurred to me. (*Pause*) Are you here with your family, Debbie?

**Debbie** No. Long holidays *en famille*, they went first.

**Michael** Debbie's father had some bad luck. He was a name at Lloyd's. Lost nearly everything.

**Anna** Oh, I am sorry.

**Debbie** It happened. A fact of life. You can't go back and undo it.

**Anna** No, but just the same, such a misfortune ...

**Debbie** Not entirely misfortune. He could have taken out insurance against losses. My mother always wanted him to, but he wouldn't listen. He said it was a waste of money, there was no risk. Only, of course, there was. It's been very hard for them to adjust; "if only", all that. I wish there was something I could do, but ... at least they're still together. Sort of.

**Anna** (*after a pause, looking at the house*) Is that him moving about?

*Michael listens*

**Michael** I can't hear anything.

**Anna** No. Is your hotel agreeable?

**Michael** I've taken an apartment. More convenient.

**Anna** Oh, yes. Much.

*Anna hears the door opening*

(*To Michael*) You see? I was right.

*Ralph comes into the courtyard/patio closing the door behind him. Ralph is in his seventies. His bearing is erect although his movements are deliberate and rather stiff. His features are still good and firm — you can see why he was a ladies' man — though his eyes can grow remote from time to time. In short, Ralph looks the part of the distinguished man in old age. However, always a pretty self-centred man, age and events have accentuated this aspect of him, and he can be decidedly crusty and acerbic. Occasional spasms of quite severe pain do not improve his temper. The only sign of these spasms is a tightening of the facial muscles. He has not told Anna about the pain, and does not intend to. As yet, the spasms pass off fairly quickly. He is wearing a large, floppy hat, his short-sleeved shirt is worn loose outside his slacks*

*Michael gets up to go and meet him. When Michael shakes hands with him, we might feel that Ralph's handshake is on the fragile side*

**Michael** Hallo. Anna said you were pretty well. You're looking good.

**Ralph** Am I?

**Michael** How are you feeling?

**Ralph** One thing I've learnt. When people ask how you're feeling, all they
want to hear is "fine". If you start telling them how you feel, their eyes glaze
over.

**Michael** Mine won't. How are you feeling?

*Debbie rises*

**Ralph** Fine. (*His eyes settle on Debbie*) Who's this?

**Michael** Someone I've brought along to meet you. (*Turning to Debbie*)
Debbie, this is Ralph.

*Debbie, with a smile, moves towards Ralph for a handshake*

**Debbie** Hallo, Ralph.

*Ralph turns and ambles away, leaving Debbie stranded*

**Ralph** We've met.

**Michael** When?

**Ralph** Now. We've just met.

*Ralph is now passing Anna's chair*

**Anna** Would you like anything, darling?

**Ralph** Yes. A large brandy.

**Anna** (*to the others*) He does this to annoy me.

**Ralph** You said "anything". Do I get one?

**Anna** No.

**Ralph** Right. So you don't mean "anything", do you.

*Ralph continues in the direction of the couch which is out in the sun*

**Anna** You'll be in the sun there. Come and sit in the shade.

**Ralph** I've been in the shade all afternoon.

*Ralph sits on the couch, removed from the others, facing them. His arrival
has not lightened the general awkwardness. For his part, Ralph is put out to
find Debbie there. Her presence interferes with the important matter he had
in mind. Anna usually tolerates or ignores Ralph's ill humours, unless he
touches on one of her vulnerable points. She cares for and about him, the man
— her man. While respecting what he does, she was never impressed by the
image, seeing through that to the man beneath*

**Anna**  You shouldn't work so hard.

**Ralph**  I don't.

**Anna**  Yes, you do. You tire yourself out when you should not, and need not. You've no deadline to work to.

**Ralph**  Oh, yes, I have. The ultimate deadline.

**Anna**  That will do, Ralph. I don't want to listen to any more of your nonsense. I mean it, Ralph. (*To the others*) It's always the same with him. The elation of creation, and depression when he stops.

**Ralph**  How would you know? You've never done it.

**Anna**  Well, I feel like something cool and refreshing. Michael?

**Michael**  Please.

**Anna**  (*standing up*) Debbie? There's wine chilling if you prefer.

**Debbie**  Whatever you're having. (*She stands up*) Can I do anything?

**Ralph**  Yes. Go and help her.

**Anna**  (*to Debbie*) You sit down and stay where you are. Everything's ready. It won't take a moment. (*To Ralph*) And you — you behave yourself.

*Anna moves towards the house. Ralph speaks just before she reaches it*

**Ralph**  Now I'm old, she thinks she can bully me with impunity.

*Anna pauses*

**Anna**  If you weren't like a wilful child, I wouldn't have to.

**Ralph**  Whatever happened to free will? I thought you were supposed to believe in free will.

*Anna decides to ignore this, and goes inside the house*

It's just as well I'm a tolerant and forgiving man. She's power mad.

**Debbie**  I think she's wonderful.

**Ralph**  Do you really. After all of a few minutes.

**Debbie**  I liked her on sight.

**Ralph**  You tend to like people on sight, quite often, do you?

**Debbie**  Sometimes. Or dislike them.

*Ralph gives her a bleak look*

**Ralph**  We have something in common. (*To Michael*) You're a damn difficult man to get hold of. You weren't at your flat, I didn't know where you were.

**Michael**  I left a message on my answerphone.

**Ralph**  I wanted to talk to you, not a machine. In the end, I had to get on to your agent.

**Michael** That was what the message said. To contact my agent. You should have listened.

**Ralph** Then your agent was in one meeting after another, or not back from lunch. It took an eternity.

**Michael** Not quite, or I wouldn't be here, would I. Well? You were very insistent. There was some particular reason, I take it?

**Ralph** (*aware of Debbie's presence*) There was ... yes ...

**Michael** Next week would have been better for me. Why wouldn't that do?

**Ralph** Because it wouldn't.

**Michael** Before Sunday. You made a point of that.

**Ralph** Yes.

**Michael** Why?

**Ralph** Because on Sunday, I have to make a decision.

*Anna appears with a tray on which are four glasses of iced, fruit-decorated drinks together with a flask or jug for refills*

*Michael is up at once*

**Anna** (*to Ralph*) A decision about what?

**Ralph** Whether to leave you, mainly.

**Anna** Oh, is that all.

**Michael** (*taking the tray from Anna*) Let me, Anna ... (*During the following he hands Debbie a drink*)

**Anna** Thank you, Michael.

**Ralph** Escape from my prison at last.

**Anna** Yes, all right. (*About their surroundings*) Only let's have the rest of the summer in this little paradise of ours, shall we?

**Ralph** Paradise, if it exists, is in the next world, if that exists.

*Michael now hands a glass to Anna*

**Anna** You'd imagine a clever man could have organized his escape long before now, wouldn't you?

*Ralph takes his drink from Michael, who then resumes his seat*

**Ralph** Success is within my grasp, you'll see.

**Anna** (*to Debbie*) This is his idea of humour, you know.

**Debbie** Is it really. I did rather wonder.

**Anna** I'm cast as the nagging wife——

**Ralph** You are.

**Anna** — and he the long suffering victim. He doesn't realize that people who don't know him might think he means it ——

**Ralph** I give up. It's hopeless.

**Anna** — whereas really he shows off in company, like a small boy.

**Ralph** Anna, you're beginning to annoy me.

**Anna** (*to the others*) I knew a surgeon once, a truly great surgeon. As a man, he wasn't nice at all, especially to his wife ——

**Ralph** Perhaps he had one like you.

**Anna** And yet he saved so many lives; with his patients, he was quite different. Ralph is like that. He pours the best of himself, insight, compassion, into his work. And you can see it. I think so, anyway. (*Addressing Debbie*) If you've seen any of his films, I'm sure you know what I mean.

**Debbie** Well, I have seen one. With Michael. It was on television. I thought it was quite good, but somehow I felt there was something missing.

**Ralph** She thought it was quite good. On television! Ye gods.

**Anna** Ralph, it's years since your last film was released.

**Ralph** A disaster. The front office morons had it re-edited.

**Michael** That was the one we saw.

**Ralph** Yes, it would be. The "something missing" was on the cutting-room floor.

**Anna** The best ones, she'd have been very young. Or not even born.

**Debbie** Michael's going to get some videos of the good ones, so that I can see them.

**Ralph** Oh, good.

*Anna's eyes meet Ralph's. An unspoken message passes between them*

**Anna** Debbie, would you like me to show you the house?

**Debbie** Yes, please. I would.

*Debbie stands up at once, as does Anna. They move towards the house*

**Anna** (*as they move*) The living-room at the back looks out across the valley. Not another house in sight. And we have much more land than you would imagine from here, with a little stream even ...

*Debbie and Anna go into the house. Anna closes the door*

*There is a moment of awkward silence. Michael stands to offer a refill*

**Michael** (*about the drinks*) Some more?

**Ralph** (*standing up*) No. What are you doing in Rome anyway? Your agent mumbles.

**Michael** I'm working at the Studio on the *Via Flaminia*.

**Ralph** What, that international blockbuster TV mini series they're shooting?

**Michael** That's it.

**Ralph** Let me guess. You've got the obligatory suntanned American, the debonair but foxy Englishman, the sophisticated Frenchman, all rich, all retarded ——

**Michael** Close. Plus the German Count, oh yes, and the Japanese geisha and her tormented banker lover. World wide sales, you know.

**Ralph** — and, I'm sure we have the breathy girls who act with their mouths open for some steamy sex scenes ...

**Michael** Plenty of those, all right. It's formula stuff, of course it is ——

**Ralph** Michael, it's unadulterated, twenty-six carat garbage. Monosyllabic, cliché scripts for a bunch of witless waxworks. Not a human being in sight. What on earth possessed you?

**Michael** The money's good.

**Ralph** Mephistopheles made much the same point to Faust, I believe.

**Michael** When you've been out of work for six months, you sympathize with Faust.

**Ralph** I've told you before, you can always come to me. I still have a few connections. I might have been able to put you up for something.

**Michael** Yes, I know, and I expect you mean well, but I'd rather not, thank you.

**Ralph** (*after a pause*) What about the novel?

**Michael** I'll finish it one day.

**Ralph** In six months, you could have done.

**Michael** I needed up-front money and for me that means writing treatments, storylines, on spec. None of them came to anything. Except this one. That led eventually to the assignment in Rome, script editing, doing rewrites — all that.

**Ralph** Hustling to write rubbish. Why grub around for hack work? You have talent. When are you going to use it, for God's sake?

**Michael** I can't pick and choose. I have to take what I can get.

**Ralph** No. A good short, simple word. You should try using it. No. Stuff your hack work.

**Michael** That's daydream time, a luxury I can't afford. Not yet. One day, yes.

**Ralph** You were doing so well. When I saw that movie you scripted at the Curzon, I thought, "Yes, damn it, he's got it. He's good".

**Michael** Written for Writers' Guild minimum. No major distribution. It didn't lead anywhere. Nothing happened.

**Ralph** So you gave up.

**Michael** Obligations came along I had to meet.

**Ralph** The divorce, you mean, I suppose.

**Michael** It set me back quite a way, yes.

**Ralph** You shouldn't have let her take you for everything you had.

**Michael** It didn't work. That was as much my fault as hers. She was entitled to a fair settlement.

**Ralph** It could have been worse, I suppose. You could have had children.

**Michael** As it happens, that was part of the problem. We couldn't.

**Ralph** You didn't tell me that.

**Michael** No, well, since we don't meet very often and you made it only too plain you didn't like her, that's hardly surprising.

**Ralph** I didn't dislike her either. You were living with her. I simply enquired why on earth you should marry her. And I was right. Look what it's cost you.

**Michael** Advice to the young, from one who knows. You certainly followed it yourself. It must have saved you a fortune in alimony over the years.

**Ralph** What? Saved me? Who do you think paid for your prep school, your public school, supported you through university? You cost me plenty, my lad.

**Michael** Of course. You paid up. You did your stuff.

**Ralph** I tried to do what was required of me, as best I could. Allow me that much at least.

**Michael** Some things can't be paid for with money.

**Ralph** (*meaning to be placatory*) Look, Michael, I don't know how we got on to this, but let's drop it. I didn't ask you to come and see me to rake over ancient grievances.

**Michael** There's something I want to know, and never asked. But I want the truth.

**Ralph** I'm not a liar. Well? Know what?

**Michael** If abortion had been readily available at the time, would I be alive now?

**Ralph** It would be better if you asked your mother.

**Michael** I'm asking you.

**Ralph** Abortion was available if you knew the right people. I knew the right people.

**Michael** Go on.

**Ralph** I thought I'd answered you.

**Michael** No.

**Ralph** Even glossy TV soaps presumably require some lowly degree of imagination. Use yours.

**Michael** I'd rather hear the good, short, simple words you like to recommend.

**Ralph** All right. Your mother deliberately set out to get pregnant. An abortion was the last thing she was after. Satisfied?

**Michael** She thought — then — you'd marry her. Is that it?

**Ralph** That's it. The truth.

**Michael** But had things been different, you'd have talked to the right people you *happened* to know.
**Ralph** I hope not. I truly hope not.

*Michael looks angry*

(*In the face of Michael's expression*) I mean that. I've always done everything I could for you.
**Michael** You were a signature on cheques. Someone I was told about. A stranger, who materialized occasionally, if and when it suited him.

*Michael's anger is for the way he feels Ralph treated his mother, the unhappiness he witnessed as a boy, not his illegitimacy. On that score his attitude to Ralph is more disdain*

**Ralph** I was trying to keep in touch. To watch you grow.
**Michael** Over odd cream teas in Petersfield? Every other speech day? Patronizing gullible dons at my college, who were impressed to find you were my father?
**Ralph** If you feel so strongly about it, write it. Damn me to hell if you like, but write it.
**Michael** Oh, I've tried, believe me.
**Ralph** The novel?
**Michael** I don't know how to finish it.
**Ralph** Perhaps, very soon, you will know. You see ... (*He hesitates*)
**Michael** Did you care about my mother at all?
**Ralph** We were together for some time. I was even faithful to her ... well, except once or twice. I must have done.
**Michael** But not enough.
**Ralph** She knew that. I made my position clear from the beginning.
**Michael** Your terms, you mean.
**Ralph** If you like. She accepted them.
**Michael** No. No, she didn't. I can still remember as a small boy, and you'd been and gone, her face as she said that perhaps, next time, you'd stay home for good.
**Ralph** We all indulge in our own private fantasies. That was hers.
**Michael** Love isn't a fantasy. She loved you. Whatever conditions you laid down, you accepted that love.
**Ralph** She knew it wasn't returned as she'd have wished. The choice was hers.
**Michael** You take don't you. But when it counts, you don't give.
**Ralph** Martyr myself to feelings I couldn't return? I'd have given her nothing but misery.

**Michael**  You did that anyway.

**Ralph**  You're judging me through a boy's eyes, but you're not a boy any more, you know life is no fairy tale. I don't expect approval, but at least try and understand.

**Michael**  I approve of and respect the work you've done. I wish I thought I could ever do anything comparable.

**Ralph**  You will. You can. But not by whoring. Leave that to those who can only write by numbers.

**Michael**  (*ignoring this*) As a man, as far as I can see, you've been a self-centred, heartless bastard.

**Ralph**  (*tiredly*) Write it, Michael. Be as bitter and unrelenting as you like. But most of all, make it so powerful, so much better than anything I've ever done, that I become a mere footnote remembered only as your father.

**Michael**  For someone who dislikes fantasies, you can purvey some beauties yourself.

**Ralph**  A fantasy that can be achieved isn't a fantasy. It's an ambition. A target. Aim for it. Do it. (*An apparent non sequitur*) Is your mother all right for money?

**Michael**  She's fine.

**Ralph**  From you? Can you afford it?

**Michael**  When you were with her, did she do paintings of cats?

**Ralph**  Yes. Not bad either, if you're sentimental about cats. I'm not. I don't like cats and cats don't like me. She stopped, when you were on the way. Why?

**Michael**  Some years ago, she started again. Began to sell them.

**Ralph**  Is there a market for that sort of stuff?

**Michael**  Oh, yes. Greetings cards at first. Then she was contracted by a chain store group. They sell her prints by the thousand.

**Ralph**  Good lord. And it pays? I mean, really pays?

**Michael**  Very well.

**Ralph**  Well, I'm damned. Good for her. Well, that's one query crossed off the agenda.

**Michael**  Agenda? Which agenda?

**Ralph**  Mine. I'm trying to settle ... (*He breaks off*)

**Anna**  (*off*) I think it's safe to join them now, don't you?

*Anna and Debbie appear from the swimming pool side*

**Michael**  (*to Ralph*) Settle what?

**Ralph**  (*quietly*) Not now. Later.

**Anna**  Have you finally stopped shouting at each other?

**Ralph**  We were not shouting. We were discussing writing in an animated fashion.

**Anna**  You were shouting.

**Ralph**  Show that girl the dried-up stream.

**Anna**  Debbie has seen the dried-up stream, which reminds me of something you said earlier. What happens Sunday?

**Ralph**  The dried-up stream reminds you of Sunday?

**Anna**  Is it to do with those furtive phone calls you've been making?

**Ralph**  They're not furtive, they're private.

**Anna**  (*to the others*) He waits until he thinks I'm not around, and makes these furtive phone calls.

**Ralph**  I don't want you listening in when I talk to my other women.

*Anna refills glasses and hands them round. Debbie resumes her seat*

**Anna**  What time is this assignation? If it's for lunch ——

**Ralph**  Anna ...

**Anna**  I need to know. Food doesn't prepare itself.

**Ralph**  You can just hob-nob with the local faithful as usual. It's nothing to do with you.

**Anna**  Ah, so you do have someone coming.

**Ralph**  None of your business. Your absence is required, not your presence.

**Anna**  It begins to sound fascinating.

**Ralph**  Anna, this is a strictly private matter. Or furtive, if you prefer.

**Anna**  Concerning what?

**Ralph**  Research. So I don't want you here.

**Anna**  For your film?

**Ralph**  What else would I be researching? Certainly not the persistence of nosy parker women. I know all about them already.

**Anna**  Well, why couldn't you say so in the first place.

**Ralph**  Because I can't stand being cross-questioned. It's like being permanently in the dock, living with you.

**Anna**  Tell Michael what you're working on. He's dying to know, aren't you Michael?

**Michael**  Oh, yes. What's the subject?

**Ralph**  Pilate.

**Debbie**  Pilot?

**Ralph**  Yes. The anatomy of a life or death decision.

**Debbie**  Sort of like *Airport*.

**Ralph**  Oh, one film has lodged in your memory then.

**Debbie**  I saw it on television.

**Ralph**  (*almost simultaneously*) On television. I guessed. No, not sort of like *Airport*. Not in the least like *Airport*.

**Debbie**  How will you make it different?

**Ralph**  Oh, quite easily, really. Pilate, Latin, Pilatus "armed with a javelin".

**Debbie**  Oh, I see. Pontius Pilate.

**Ralph**  Pontius, Latin, Pontivagus "belonging to the sea".

**Anna**  He's being funny, again.

**Ralph**  Certainly not. To my mind, Pontius Pilate has always had a very bad press.

**Anna**  A bad press? He crucified the Son of God.

**Ralph**  Anna, please. He tried every which way to avoid crucifying Him. He practically stood on his head to find a way out.

**Anna**  The fact remains that he did. Anyway, you hypocrite, you don't believe Jesus was the Son of God.

**Ralph**  That's the least difficult concept to accept.

**Anna**  Oh, really!

**Ralph**  The prayer He taught begins "Our Father". If that means anything, it means we're all the children of God. In that case of course He was the Son of God. (*About Michael*) Like him. Even me.

**Anna**  You? I don't know how you can sit there and say such things. You don't even believe in God.

**Ralph**  What the devil has that got to do with it? Completely beside the point. I'm concerned with a man, alien cultures, fanaticism.

**Michael**  How much is known about Pilate except from the New Testament?

**Ralph**  He crops up in the works of Josephus, Philo, Eusebius. Pontius Pilate was appointed governor of Judaea by the Emperor Tiberius in AD 26.

**Michael**  How do you see him? A career man? An ambitious professional?

**Ralph**  That's right. And Judaea would have been regarded as an absolute stinker of an appointment.

**Michael**  But where a man could make a name for himself.

**Anna**  He certainly managed to achieve that.

**Ralph**  Christ was crucified around AD 33. In AD 36, Pilate was recalled after a series of riots and a Samaritan uprising. He was banished to Gaul. Far from making a name for himself, he'd cocked it up. And in Gaul, Eusebius tells us, Pontius Pilate took his own life.

**Debbie**  Why? Guilt? Remorse for what he'd done?

**Ralph**  Well, he was claimed as a saint by the Ethiopian Church.

**Anna**  I think you've just made that up.

**Ralph**  According to Coptic tradition, Pontius Pilate was martyred as a Christian. (*To Michael*) Well? What do you think?

**Michael**  I think I like it.

**Anna**  I think it sounds blasphemous.

**Ralph**  It wouldn't be blasphemous at all.

**Anna**  If an unbeliever turns our Lord God Jesus Christ into a character in a film, invents dialogue for Him, purports to see into His mind, as far as I'm concerned, that's blasphemy.

**Ralph**  You can't see into my mind, woman, so don't make stupid assumptions.

**Michael**  How would you approach it then?

**Ralph**  Translate it to another time, another place. The British Empire under Queen Victoria.

**Michael**  The story of a man, forced to do something he knows is wrong. A latter day Pontius Pilate. Trapped by his role, his background, the society he lives in. There but for the grace of God go most of us.

**Ralph**  The parallels will be there. (*Eyeing Michael*) All kinds of parallels. (*At Anna*) But no Jesus. No blasphemy.

**Michael**  Shot on location?

**Ralph**  Of course.

**Michael**  It sounds expensive. You're talking about an awful lot of noughts. Are you still able to get access to that kind of finance?

**Ralph**  Fashions change. You don't notice at first. Except, you don't hear from people you thought were your friends. Projects get turned down. The phone goes quiet. You realize you're out. I think most people assume I'm already dead. Or in my dotage.

**Anna**  Your world always was full of exceptionally silly people.

**Ralph**  Now the pendulum may have reversed its swing to include me back in.

**Michael**  You've had an approach?

**Ralph**  The money's there. Some of it's in my bank account already. We go as soon as — (*a gesture towards his work room*) — it's ready.

*Debbie smothers a half-yawn*

**Ralph**  (*to Debbie*) Are we boring you? Or taxing you unduly?

**Debbie**  No. Had a late night. (*To Anna*) How did you two ever get together?

**Ralph**  A question which has baffled many great minds, including mine.

**Anna**  Oh, he was filming on location in Vienna. He had a serious heart attack. He nearly died. I was a Coronary Care Nurse at the hospital.

**Debbie**  The hospital romance routine? Devoted nurse? Smitten patient? Like on television.

**Anna**  An awful cliché, I know, but there it is. It does happen in the real world too.

**Ralph**  I'd never been ill before in my life. I'd enjoyed perfect health and fitness.

**Anna**  Nonsense, you chain-smoked, and you were a heavy drinker.

**Ralph**  I was in my fifties, temporarily unattached, suddenly laid low, still not quite believing death had passed me by, weak, vulnerable. She saw her chance and pounced on her helpless prey.

**Anna**  In fact, it was all rather romantic.

**Ralph**  Oh, Gawd ...

**Anna**  We practically had to elope.

**Debbie** Really?

**Ralph** No, not really. This is the saccharine version.

**Anna** (*still to Debbie*) My family were very much against it.

**Debbie** (*pointedly*) Because he was so much *older* than you?

*Ralph gives her a hostile look*

**Anna** In Austria, an older man was regarded as quite suitable for a husband. And of course, he was rather famous. No, it was his reputation as a womanizer.

**Ralph** Oh, happy days.

**Anna** Austrians expected a man to be experienced before marriage, of course. That's one thing. But a libertine like him was too much for my family.

**Ralph** Libertine. No-one says libertine except foreigners with dictionaries.

**Anna** "But Anna," they said to me. "He's such a terrible old goat". Well, he was, of course, but I knew I could tether him.

**Ralph** So, that's how I'm regarded. As a tethered old goat.

**Anna** Not any more, darling. You were quite easy to house train.

**Debbie** Were women expected to be experienced too?

**Anna** Well, Vienna, a big hospital, young doctors, it wasn't a nunnery. Friendships could lead to something closer. Even a few proposals of marriage I seem to recall.

**Ralph** If only you'd accepted one of them.

**Anna** They weren't for me, darling.

**Debbie** But he was.

**Ralph** She is endeavouring, with very little success, to restrain her incredulity.

**Anna** Are you staying in Rome for long, Debbie?

**Debbie** No, more of a short break. Back to work next week.

**Ralph** Oh, you work? You have a proper job?

**Debbie** Yes.

**Ralph** For whom? If one may enquire?

**Debbie** Some friends of mine.

**Ralph** Who are engaged in? These friends?

**Debbie** They organize business conferences all over Europe.

**Ralph** Oh, yes. I've endured those in my time. (*To Michael*) You too, perhaps.

**Michael** Just one.

**Ralph** (*to Debbie*) And you are employed as?

**Debbie** I look after the hospitality side.

**Ralph** In my day, a smiling, attractive young lady would accost one in the bar, offer drinks, be most agreeable. Even solicitous you might say. Something of that sort?

**Debbie** People arrive. They may not know anyone. We put them at ease, look after them, effect introductions.

**Ralph** And be nice to them.

**Debbie** I'm not paid to be nasty to them.

**Ralph** Of course not. You're a professional hostess. So Michael arrived, you were nice to him, and now you've taken a short break to continue to be nice to him out of hours, as it were.

**Anna** Ralph, for goodness' sake ——

**Debbie** It's quite all right, Anna.

**Anna** It's not all right at all.

**Debbie** I hear worse than that on duty.

**Ralph** Worse than what? I merely proffered a job description.

**Debbie** I'd like to leave now, Michael, if you please.

*Debbie stands up, advances, and confronts Ralph, dominating the stage*

I am not being paid to listen to this boring, pretentious, old fart.

*Michael stands up. During the following, Anna rises*

**Michael** I shouldn't have brought you. My mistake. Sorry. Let's go. Anna, nothing to do with you ...

**Ralph** Michael, don't, there are things I need to say.

**Michael** You've said all I ever want to hear from you.

**Ralph** God damn it, I didn't ask you to bring this bimbo with you.

**Michael** Debbie, come on, before I ——

**Ralph** Michael ——

**Michael** Shut up. Just shut up.

*Ralph recoils from Michael's anger. Debbie takes Anna's hand*

**Debbie** Ich nehme an dass wir uns nicht mehr entgegnen werden. Ich bedanke mich fur Ihre Libenswurdigkeit. (I don't suppose we shall meet again. Thank you for your kindness.) Je ne peux pas croire comment vous puissiez supporter un sale égoiste pareil. (How you tolerate such a disagreeable, self-centred egotist, I do not know.)

**Ralph** (*helplessly*) Michael ... Michael ...

**Michael** (*on the move*) Goodbye, Anna — sorry.

*Debbie leaves through the gate, followed by Michael*

**Ralph** Anna, do something, stop him.

**Anna** Don't be so ridiculous. It's already done. And you did it.

*Ralph sits down limply on the couch. Anna looks at him with dry amusement.*
*The sound of car doors slamming, off, the engine starting, the car driving*
*away*

She told me, in her fluent French ——
**Ralph** I know what she told you.
**Anna** — she said she didn't know how I tolerated such a disagreeable, self-
centred, egotist. A bimbo indeed.
**Ralph** All right. But she's a show off. She was showing off at my expense.
**Anna** Which you deserved. She paid you back in your own coin, and quite
right too. What on earth came over you?

*Ralph shakes his head helplessly*

**Ralph** She was here. As soon as I saw her, I knew it had all gone wrong, it
would turn into a social occasion, you'd make endless conversation, and
I wouldn't get the chance ... (*He breaks off*)
**Anna** To do what?

*Ralph is sunk in misery*

**Ralph** I wanted to talk to Michael alone.
**Anna** I know that. Why do you think I took her off? You had plenty of time
with Michael, but all you did was quarrel.
**Ralph** (*wretchedly*) I got sidetracked. My thoughts aren't as coherent as they
used to be. I lose the thread. I can't think in a straight line, the way I used
to.
**Anna** What a feeble excuse. Your mind is as sharp as it ever was.
**Ralph** (*shaking his head*) No ...
**Anna** Oh, yes. You just decided to be nasty and now, because you haven't
had your own way, you sit there sulking, feeling sorry for yourself.
**Ralph** I'm not feeling sorry for myself. I'm miserable.
**Anna** Serves you right. I've no sympathy with you. You shouldn't
misbehave. (*Pause*) I suppose it's time for tea.
**Ralph** I don't want any tea.
**Anna** I wasn't asking you. You don't deserve any.
**Ralph** Oh, bugger off woman, and leave me alone.

*Anna moves towards the house, pauses, looks back at him, smiling*

**Anna** (*with a chuckle*) A boring, pretentious old fart. What a nice girl. I like
her.

*Anna goes into the house*

*Ralph is left, sitting*

*Black-out*

SCENE 2

*The same. Evening. The same day*

*Darkness has fallen. Faint moonlight bathes the house. The courtyard/patio is illuminated by a lamp over the gate, and another elsewhere, leaving patches of shadow here and there*

*When the Lights come up, the sun umbrella (if used) is down. Ralph is sitting brooding beside the table. He has changed his clothes for the evening. On the table is a tea cup*

*After a few moments, Anna comes out of the house, moves until she is behind Ralph, bends, puts her arms round him and rests her cheek against his*

**Anna**  Feeling better?
**Ralph**  No.
**Anna**  More tea?
**Ralph**  No.
**Anna**  Would you like me to go away?

*Ralph pats her hands with one of his*

**Ralph**  No.
**Anna**  I phoned Michael. His machine answered, so I left a message. Do you think he'll call back?
**Ralph**  No.
**Anna**  It that all you're going to say to me? No?
**Ralph**  No. (*Pause*) Let go. You're giving me a crick in my neck.

*Anna sits down near him*

**Anna**  That's better. When you complain, I know you're improving.
**Ralph**  At my time of life, I'm not going to improve.
**Anna**  Yes, you are. Of course, you are. Were you serious about Pontius Pilate?

**Ralph** M'm? Oh, yes.

**Anna** Why?

**Ralph** Why not?

**Anna** It's out of character.

**Ralph** Whose?

**Anna** Yours. No matter how you write it, you will have to deal with beliefs you've never held. And don't tell me I'm wrong.

**Ralph** You're not.

**Anna** Well, then. Tell me.

**Ralph** It's hard to know where to start.

**Anna** Whenever someone says that, you snort, and say "try starting at the beginning".

**Ralph** If I do, don't jump to conclusions.

**Anna** I never jump to conclusions. What do you mean?

**Ralph** Well, then, the beginning, the seeds which grew into that lack of belief.

**Anna** I know that. You're too arrogant. Too superior. You think you know everything.

**Ralph** (*a weary look at Anna*) That, woman, is what I mean. You jump before I've even bloody started.

**Anna** Sorry, go on. I'll just sit here and say nothing.

**Ralph** When I was a boy, we moved house. A new neighbour, Peter, ran a Sunday School. My mother sent me there.

**Anna** You? Sunday School?

*Anna meets his gaze*

Sorry.

**Ralph** (*back in the past*) It was a drab hall. Belonged to the Ancient Order of Foresters. Smelt of stale buns and stewed tea. Not a church school. Christian something. I forget. An old upright piano. Hymns, prayers, Bible reading.

**Anna** (*after a pause, prompting*) And I suppose you played truant.

**Ralph** No. There were girls at Sunday School.

**Anna** Girls? How old were you for goodness' sake?

**Ralph** Old enough to suspect that girls were different. Puberty arrived early in my case.

**Anna** That is not the most astounding revelation I've ever heard.

**Ralph** With head bent in prayer, you could squint sideways at the girls' class, at the white ankle socks, the young bodies, the skirts just below the knee — and speculate.

**Anna** Oh, dear. Hopeless, even then. Beyond redemption.

**Ralph** Peter thought not. He offered salvation. Repentance. Come to Jesus. Apparently, not only did I have to embrace Jesus, but my decent, harmless mother and father had to be saved too. Or they would be tortured in hell for all eternity. It was ferocious stuff.

**Anna** I don't think I like this story.

**Ralph** (*ironically*) In those bad old, primitive days, even at elementary school, in classes of forty or more, we were taught something of geography and pre-history. I knew that great civilizations had flourished and decayed long before the birth of Christ. I knew countless millions of people lived and died without ever hearing the message, the good news. I put this to the mild-mannered Peter. What happened to them? He said they had gone to hell. Condemned without being given a chance? Was that quite fair? He repeated, anyone who wasn't saved went to hell. He was very firm about it. I never went back. Better no God than that one.

**Anna** The man was a misguided fanatic. You must have realized that later on.

**Ralph** Later, came better, more rational reasons. The age-old problem of random pain, undeserved suffering, not just humans, all living creatures, predators and victims, everything founded on killing, fear, death. What kind of all-powerful being would invent anything so cruel?

**Anna** I try not to think what a distance there is between us, Ralph. It makes me sad.

**Ralph** You've lived with my disbelief, though.

**Anna** Yes, from the beginning, when you wouldn't marry me in church. You've lived with a heart condition. That doesn't mean you like it.

**Ralph** I couldn't utter words I didn't believe.

**Anna** No, you have such integrity, such high-minded convictions.

**Ralph** Some things those convictions failed to explain. The very concept of beauty. A perception taken for granted but quite inexplicable in rational terms. The number and variety of religions, right back to early man. Were they all a search for something unknowable? Not that such questions troubled me much. But recently ... (*He breaks off*)

**Anna** What happened recently?

**Ralph** I became acutely aware of my own mortality, the end near at hand.

**Anna** You've many good years left before you yet. I shall see to that.

**Ralph** The final mystery ... Einstein said, "something deeply hidden has to be behind things". A haunting phrase.

**Anna** It needn't be all that deeply hidden.

**Ralph** Such certainty. How easy it is for you.

**Anna** It's not easy at all. Sometimes it's very difficult to believe in God.

**Ralph** You have doubts? You?

**Anna** "Faith which does not doubt is dead faith."

**Ralph** Dead faith?

**Anna** Not my words. From *The Agony of Christianity*.

**Ralph** Dead faith. I like it. Perhaps it's a human failing. Science is certainly afflicted with it. Butterflies fluttering in China cause thunderstorms over New York months later, we were told. This is why they cannot predict if it will rain next week, but yet they *can* tell us what the world temperature and sea level will be in thirty years' time. Aren't they clever! But is there not some small contradiction here? Perhaps it's those butterflies again. They elevate their ignorance, their dead faith, into the chaos theory. Then we have the Big Bang, which occurred fifteen billion years ago, or perhaps twenty billion, or possibly only eight billion. The great minds differ slightly. Anyway, give or take several thousand million years, there was an explosion of incomprehensible magnitude. Gigantic clouds of violently expanding gases, eventually coalesced into a myriad stars, the countless galaxies, we call the universe. The theoretical physicists refer to this event as "a singularity". Well, yes. Quite singular, really. The arrival of a universe. If you say, "OK, fine, but what about *before* the Big Bang?", they explain that time, space and matter emerged simultaneously. Since time itself did not exist, there was no "before", and therefore your question has no meaning. Or, perhaps, it has no answer. With teams of great brains, banks of computers, space telescopes and all the rest, what has science come up with? The first few verses of Genesis!

**Anna** (*quoting*) "And the earth was without form and void; and darkness was upon the face of the deep. And God said, Let there be light."

**Anna** }
**Ralph** } (*together*) "And there was light."

**Ralph** Briefer, more elegantly put, but it comes to the same thing.

**Anna** And this has led you — where?

**Ralph** To Pontius Pilate. A man who recognized, but could not understand. If I could reason my way into his mind as he confronted the inexplicable ... a kind of parallel ... do you see?

**Anna** I see you being contradictory, as usual.

**Ralph** I thought I was being eminently reasonable.

**Anna** That's what's contradictory. After a lifetime of disbelief because you said such belief was irrational, now you want to reason your way into believing. You can't. It's not like that.

**Ralph** A blind man fumbling in a strange room can only try and reason out the nature of his surroundings.

**Anna** God is beyond reason. All you have to do is accept. He won't mind you being late.

**Ralph** The act of faith. I can't. Only grope, in my own way.

**Anna** Like a blind man. But you're not blind. You just refuse to turn on the light.

**Ralph** I can't find the switch. But "Something deeply hidden" is there, yes. Although ... (*He breaks off*)

**Anna** (*after a pause*) Your something deeply hidden, does that suggest life after death to you?

**Ralph** Consciousness, the mind, is so extraordinary, even in the least of us. When it comes to a Beethoven, a Shakespeare, a Michael Angelo, ordinary fallible mortals ... yet touched by such transcendent gifts ... I wonder if some form of consciousness ... (*It is left hanging in mid air*)

**Anna** Go on.

**Ralph** There's no more.

**Anna** Well, I shall pray for you.

**Ralph** Don't. Please.

**Anna** You can't stop me. Besides, I do anyway. All the time.

**Ralph** There is one gift I would like.

**Anna** What? I'll include it, unless it's something awful.

**Ralph** At the point of death, even if nothing follows but ... nothing — a moment of understanding, of illumination ... I'd like that.

**Anna** Oh, well, I shan't bother to include that. You're not going to die.

**Ralph** We're all going to die. Simple arithmetic says I shall die long before you.

**Anna** I can't stand it when you get morbid.

**Ralph** Face it, Anna. Do the sums.

**Anna** I'll face it if and when I have to. That's for the future.

**Ralph** The future arrives. It always arrives.

**Anna** Are you suddenly gifted with clairvoyance? You don't know what lies ahead. None of us do. People get killed on the roads every day. I could have an accident driving into Rome. Or even to church. You might be the one left alone. Who knows? Good God, are we supposed to live in fear and dread?

**Ralph** Whatever you say, it's still odds on I shall go first. It could happen any time. It could be soon. I'd feel better if I thought you were prepared for that. If you were ready, eyes open, instead of avoiding the subject, every time I try and talk about it. I'm concerned for you, Anna. Having to leave you alone one day.

*Anna stands up, angry, and with some bitterness*

**Anna** Concerned for me? You? Why? If I'd had children, I wouldn't be left alone. You stopped me.

**Ralph** You knew I didn't want children. I was too old for all that.

**Anna** You stopped me. So you're all I have. You made sure of that.

*With which, Anna turns towards the house*

**Ralph** Anna ...

**Anna** You're a wicked, selfish old man. I don't want to talk to you any more.

*Anna goes inside the house*

**Ralph** (*to himself, sadly*) Oh, Anna ... (*A cry of despair*) Anna ...

*Black-out*

SCENE 3

*The same. The following Sunday morning*

*A fairly fat envelope lies on the table*

*The Lights come up on Ralph, wearing different casual clothes, the same large hat, moving to the gate, listening for the sound of an approaching car*

*There is the distant sound of a car approaching. Ralph reacts. But the car turns off somewhere, the engine note dies away, leaving only summer silence. Ralph turns away, disappointed. After a moment or two he senses someone behind him. Ralph swings round, looks towards the open gate, startled*

*The Visitor appears without warning. His appearance could be that of a Harley Street doctor. A sleek, handsome, fifty-plus man, he wears a dark light-weight suit, white shirt, discreet tie. He is self-possessed, reassuring, perceptive, uncomfortably so. He carries the sort of bag which could belong to a doctor. He smiles pleasantly at Ralph*

**Visitor**  Good-morning, sir.
**Ralph**  (*assessing this stranger*) Good-morning. You are?
**Visitor**  From the society. You are expecting me?
**Ralph**  Expecting someone.
**Visitor**  Me, sir. The local man, you might say.
**Ralph**  Local? You're English.
**Visitor**  So are you. But here we both are.
**Ralph**  You live here?
**Visitor**  In semi-retirement. My wife is Italian. Mine is quite passable, I'm told.
**Ralph**  I didn't hear your car.
**Visitor**  I left it at the bottom of the hill.
**Ralph**  You prefer your visits to remain secret.
**Visitor**  Private and confidential, sir. Most clients prefer that, I find. (*He looks round, carefully*) Are we alone?
**Ralph**  My wife has driven into the village for Mass. We shan't be disturbed.

**Visitor** Might I ask how you came to contact the society?
**Ralph** A friend had dealt with them on behalf of a relative.
**Visitor** Information for research purposes, I believe you said.
**Ralph** Yes.
**Visitor** It's a great pleasure to meet you, sir. I've always much enjoyed your films.
**Ralph** Thank you.
**Visitor** And I much admired the novel. The man in mid-life, disillusioned, an inventor, his ideals corrupted by commercialism, weary of loveless affairs.
**Ralph** You have a good memory. That was a long time ago.
**Visitor** May I ask if that was autobiographical, to some extent?
**Ralph** No. Imagination. I've never been an inventor.
**Visitor** You've invented a good deal in your time. That tantalizing ending. The young woman he meets. Did she change him? Did they become lovers? In the book you leave us there.
**Ralph** It felt right to let the reader decide.
**Visitor** The film version was more explicit, I recall. True love, a happy ending.
**Ralph** A film is a different animal.
**Visitor** I preferred the way it was in the book.
**Ralph** The money men thought the open ending risked leaving the audience dissatisfied. It was a high-budget movie.
**Visitor** Somehow it felt like a compromise.
**Ralph** Only if you'd read the book.
**Visitor** True.
**Ralph** Most of the audience wouldn't have. It was the only way I could get it made.
**Visitor** I remember asking my bookseller to send me any more of your books but ——
**Ralph** That was the only one.
**Visitor** Why was that? Other commitments?
**Ralph** It was the only subject I ever felt the need to write as a novel.
**Visitor** Because it was a more personal piece?
**Ralph** I didn't analyse it. It was a feeling.
**Visitor** Film-maker, director, screenwriter. You turn your hand to just one novel, and that a bestseller. You're a polymath, sir.
**Ralph** I also become bored quite rapidly with small talk.
**Visitor** There is a consultation fee. I take it that was mentioned.

*Ralph indicates the envelope*

Ah. Thank you. *(He picks up the fat envelope and swiftly checks the notes inside)*

**Ralph**  Your services are only available to those who can afford it, I gather.

**Visitor**  The society adopts something of a Robin Hood attitude. Were you in financial difficulty, there would be no fee. Are you?

**Ralph**  Are you? (*He waves the question away dismissively*)

**Visitor**  Your generosity will subsidize those who need help, but lack the means. (*He places the envelope on the table*)

**Ralph**  What do I call you? (*Pause*) Well? Speak up. How do the people you deal with refer to you?

**Visitor**  Labels open up a gulf, I always feel.

**Ralph**  So do charlatans. Or those with a shady past. Is that it? Disgraced, were you? Forced to live abroad? What was it? Drink? Women? Swindling old ladies? Malpractice? What?

**Visitor**  An aggressive attitude usually signals defensive feelings. Or is it merely the result of your low boredom threshold?

**Ralph**  (*pointing at the envelope*) That says I'm entitled to know what qualifies you to offer me advice.

**Visitor**  Oh, a reference? Well, a reasonably successful career in my own field. But I came to believe that life at all costs is a modern heresy. We cheerfully prevent life, abortions by the hundred thousand annually, but once born, life is sacrosanct. For most, rightly so. For some, a mockery. They ask for relief, the right to make their own decision. It is withheld. Wrongly, I thought, but at the time I could do nothing. Now through the society, in my semi-retirement, relieved of previous constraints, I can. Anything else you feel you should know?

**Ralph**  You've told me. It's possible. It can be arranged. Tell me how.

**Visitor**  First, comes a case assessment. (*He picks up the envelope and tucks it away in a jacket pocket*) Personality. Mental state. Reasons.

**Ralph**  It's only a character in a piece of fiction, for God's sake.

**Visitor**  Let us strive for authenticity, even so. It's not available off the shelf, like cheese in a supermarket. Describe him or her for me.

**Ralph**  Him.

**Visitor**  Age?

**Ralph**  Elderly.

**Visitor**  Senile?

**Ralph**  Certainly not! (*He modifies his tone*) It wouldn't be right, dramatically.

**Visitor**  No. All his faculties intact.

**Ralph**  Yes and no.

**Visitor**  Which?

**Ralph**  He's aware they are ... fading.

**Visitor**  Lapses in concentration? Failing memory? Loses the thread sometimes?

**Ralph**  Not all the time. Occasionally. But ... fading.

**Visitor** He resents growing old.

**Ralph** Not the passage of years. The gradual loss of ability.

**Visitor** Physical ability?

**Ralph** He could live with that.

**Visitor** Intellectual powers.

**Ralph** It's a complex equation.

**Visitor** Health problems too?

**Ralph** Heart.

**Visitor** Long standing?

**Ralph** Yes. Open heart surgery not so long ago.

**Visitor** And these are the reasons you have given this character you have in mind.

**Ralph** His motives. As I see them.

**Visitor** Is he a religious man?

**Ralph** Not in the formal sense. He's conscious of "something deeply hidden". But what, no. He can't see it.

**Visitor** Are this person's worldly affairs in order?

**Ralph** Everything's prepared. Will updated, bequests ... to make it all as smooth as possible.

**Visitor** After the event.

**Ralph** Yes. So what I need to know is, the methods you would recommend.

**Visitor** What comes to mind in this hypothetical case is that he will be taking drugs, in which case ——

**Ralph** (*interrupting*) No, not drugs. Nothing like that.

**Visitor** Purely out of interest, why not?

**Ralph** His wife gives him his drugs.

**Visitor** He must have access. Presumably she doesn't keep them under lock and key.

**Ralph** She's meticulous. She'd notice. If she even suspected he had ended his own life, it would cause her ... distress.

**Visitor** She is, what? A Catholic?

**Ralph** He needs another way.

**Visitor** I see.

**Ralph** Veterinary surgeons do it all the time.

**Visitor** They don't risk being accused of murder.

**Ralph** So it can be done.

**Visitor** It can.

**Ralph** How?

**Visitor** A simple injection.

**Ralph** Pain?

**Visitor** No. Just sleep.

**Ralph** In? How long?

**Visitor** Seconds. All over.

**Ralph** And since no-one knows he's met someone like you, there's very little risk of anyone being accused of murder, is there.

**Visitor** However, in a case like this ——

**Ralph** Such a service would be expensive. He's prepared for that.

**Visitor** I was about to say that, in the case you have outlined, I would advise counselling.

**Ralph** Counselling?

**Visitor** Counselling.

**Ralph** He's made his decision. He doesn't want bloody counselling.

**Visitor** The trouble with this decision is that it's irreversible.

**Ralph** He doesn't want it reversed.

**Visitor** I'm not convinced of that.

**Ralph** You?! You're not?! (*Controlling himself*) He's a rational man. He's thought it through. *He's* convinced. That's all that matters.

**Visitor** He's convinced himself, I accept that. (*Gazing at Ralph*) The man I see, the one you've put to me, has problems, yes, but he may have them out of proportion. He's turned inward upon himself. His despair may be temporary.

**Ralph** And a few counselling sessions ...

**Visitor** It's well worth trying.

**Ralph** At an appropriate fee ...

**Visitor** Little enough for an acceptable life extension.

**Ralph** He doesn't want it extended. How many more times.

**Visitor** He might. After a few weeks.

**Ralph** Or months?

**Visitor** Perhaps. See how it goes.

**Ralph** As a technical adviser, you're completely useless.

**Visitor** Quite likely. I don't deal in fiction much, you see.

**Ralph** Perhaps we need to ice the cake a little.

*Ralph takes a typed letter from his shirt pocket, unfolds it. The letter comprises two or three short paragraphs*

I did some previous research, talked to my GP.

*He hands the visitor the copy of a diagnosis he'd received from a consultant. The Visitor looks at Ralph, then reads the letter without any change of expression*

Quite a good authority, I'm told.

**Visitor** A first-class man. I knew him when he was at Guy's.

*He holds out the letter to Ralph. Ralph does not take it*

**Ralph** (*drily*) For your tiles.

*The Visitor pockets the letter*

Still set on counselling?

**Visitor** It would depend. Sometimes, when people feel very sorry for themselves, naturally enough ...

**Ralph** He doesn't. No "Rage, rage, against the dying of the light".

**Visitor**         "Do not go gentle into that good night,
            Old age should burn and rave at close of day;
            Rage, rage against the dying of the light."

**Ralph** What did he know? He died before he was forty. A rather silly piece of juvenile peevish bravado. When you get old, you're not afraid to die. You're afraid you won't die in time.

**Visitor** In this case, perhaps, from a greater poet who made it into his sixties, "calm of mind, all passion spent"?

**Ralph** Well, he might not go quite that far. But ready.

**Visitor** You present a nice predicament, sir.

**Ralph** The risk factor?

**Visitor** It does exist. For the expert concerned. I expect he would look for ——

**Ralph** Insurance against the risk. A premium.

*Ralph moves and retrieves a small leather bag, previously concealed in (say) a plant pot. He hands it to the Visitor*

Like this, perhaps.

*The Visitor opens the bag. Inside are bundles of notes*

**Visitor** You do like to place your faith in the power of money, don't you.

**Ralph** A donation for Robin Hood, to use for the needy. Enough?

**Visitor** More than adequate. Generous. *(He closes the bag and places it on the table)* Doubtless you will wish to reflect.

**Ralph** No.

**Visitor** It would be no trouble, indeed preferable, to call again in a day or two.

**Ralph** Now. Do it now.

**Visitor** Your wife ——

**Ralph** Better for her this way. Believe me. I know.

**Visitor** You are absolutely, completely certain?

**Ralph** Yes.

**Visitor** Very well. Sit down, please.

*Ralph sits on a chair beside the table, the Visitor opens his bag. He swabs Ralph's lower arm. He takes out a hypodermic and fills it from an ampoule. During this process, Ralph studies his Visitor's face*

**Ralph** When you despatch people like this ...
**Visitor** Very rarely like this. Usually it is a matter of offering advice on the best means.
**Ralph** Well, facilitate their departure.
**Visitor** I suppose I can't challenge that.
**Ralph** Where do you think you're sending them?
**Visitor** Do I believe in an afterlife, you mean?
**Ralph** Yes.
**Visitor** Like Jung, "I know — that I do not know."
**Ralph** You don't deny the possibility.
**Visitor** To deny what I cannot know would seem to me to be remarkably arrogant. And you?
**Ralph** Much the same. Although the prospect of eternal life ... this one can be boring enough sometimes ... but passing the time throughout eternity ... I don't know.
**Visitor** But surely, an afterlife, if there is one, can only exist outside time. Boredom arises when time hangs heavy, but if there is no time ...
**Ralph** Yes, I suppose that's right. Well, I shall soon know. Or not, as the case may be.
**Visitor** We could continue this discussion on Monday, if you wish.
**Ralph** Will you have a definitive answer by then?
**Visitor** No.
**Ralph** No point in waiting then. (*He holds out his arm*) Thank you for making it easy.
**Visitor** The merest pin prick.
**Ralph** I know. I've had plenty.
**Visitor** Ready?
**Ralph** Yes.

*Ralph closes his eyes. The Visitor gives him the injection*

**Visitor** Count backwards from ten.
**Ralph** Nine ... eight ... seven ... (*slowing*) ... six ... five ... (*his voice dies*)

*Ralph's head falls backwards. His body slumps. The Visitor carefully re-arranges the body so that Ralph's chin is on his chest and places his hat over his eyes so that Ralph appears to be asleep*

*This done, the Visitor places the small bag of money inside his own bag and walks away. He pauses to look back at Ralph before he passes through the gate and out of sight*

*For the last seconds of the scene, the Lights slowly dim to black-out — "the dying of the light"*

CURTAIN

# ACT II

## SCENE 1

*The same day. Later that morning*

*The telephone is ringing indoors. Ralph's body is in the same sleeping pose. Meantime, the sun has shifted a little, and he is now in its full glare*

*There is the sound of a car arriving off, the slam of a car door. The telephone continues to ring*

*Anna comes through the gate, dressed for Mass, wearing a hat, carrying a handbag. She sees Ralph*

**Anna** (*irritated*) Oh, dear. Not again. Ralph. Wake up.

*Anna moves on to the door of the house. The ringing inside stops. She looks back at Ralph*

Oh! Didn't you hear the telephone?

*Anna crosses to Ralph and shakes him by the shoulder*

Ralph. I'm back.

*Ralph's head lolls sideways. Anna shakes him again*

Ralph, for goodness' sake wake up, do.

*This time, Ralph lifts his head. He opens his eyes and tries to focus on Anna, blinking*

**Ralph** (*vaguely*) Anna ... is that you ...?
**Anna** Of course it's me. Who else?
**Ralph** (*still vague*) What are you doing here?
**Anna** Looking at a silly old man, that's what.
**Ralph** (*vague*) But I'm still ... what happened ...?
**Anna** I've told you before, you mustn't go to sleep in the sun. It's bad for you.

*Ralph eases himself into an upright position*

**Ralph** (*vague*) I'm supposed to be ... I thought I was ... but I'm not? ... I don't
understand.
**Anna** Really. Look at you. As if you've been drugged.

*Anna takes his arm, and looks at it*

And you've been bitten. Ah ... Move into the shade. I'll fetch something
to put on that sting. Do as you're told and move, Ralph. Come along. Get
up ...

*She helps Ralph to move sideways under the shade of the sun umbrella (or
olive tree)*

I don't know. I can't leave you alone for five minutes.

*Anna hurries into the house*

*Ralph's head is clearing, and he first gropes, and then looks around for his
small bag. Finding that it has gone, his face expresses his dawning
realization*

**Ralph** (*to himself*) The money ... gone ... (*Louder*) A high-class con man. The
cheating bastard ...
**Anna** (*off*) What did you say?

*Ralph's indignation gives way to growing amusement*

**Ralph** (*calling*) Nothing. (*To himself*) Played with me, showed me the bait,
and hooked me like a gullible old fish. (*He looks at his arm, and begins to
laugh out loud*) Bitten is right. And what can I do about it? Report him to
the police? Nothing. The perfect sting. It's wonderful. I love it. Oh, dear
... (*He is wiping tears from his eyes and shaking with laughter*)

*Anna comes out of the house, and crosses to him, carrying cotton wool and
a small bottle*

**Anna** What on earth are you laughing at?
**Ralph** (*controlling himself*) Nothing.
**Anna** Nothing is hysterically funny?
**Ralph** Yes ... oh, dear ...
**Anna** I think the sun boiled your brains.

**Ralph** No. Half-baked, that's all. (*Which nearly sets him off again*)
**Anna** Ralph, for goodness' sake ...
**Ralph** Sorry. (*He lifts his arm to wipe his eyes again*)
**Anna** Keep still. Will you do as you're told? Just for once, and keep still?

*Anna dabs his arm with the cotton wool, and looks at him suspiciously*

Well?
**Ralph** Well what?
**Anna** This hilarious joke.
**Ralph** It's too silly. I can't.
**Anna** (*inspecting the "sting"*) Perhaps I should put a dressing on it.
**Ralph** Oh, leave it. It's nothing.
**Anna** Like this joke you won't tell me. If you were laughing at me ...
**Ralph** I wasn't.
**Anna** If so, I don't like being laughed at.
**Ralph** Nothing to do with you. I promise. Cross my heart and hope to die!

*Ralph giggles then catches Anna's stony gaze*

Anna, I was laughing at myself. Is that forbidden? Have you made a new rule?
**Anna** It depends what it was about.
**Ralph** Look, I'll never laugh again. Will that satisfy you?

*Anna sits, and gazes at Ralph*

**Anna** The phone was ringing. It stopped before I could answer it.
**Ralph** I didn't hear anything.
**Anna** No, you were dead to the world, weren't you.
**Ralph** It did seem rather like that, yes.
**Anna** Didn't your visitor come?
**Ralph** Yes. I fell asleep when he left.
**Anna** Did you get what you wanted?
**Ralph** No. He turned out to be a phoney.
**Anna** Well, I hope you didn't give him any money.
**Ralph** Good lord, no. As if I would.
**Anna** You can have your swim before lunch. Wake yourself up.
**Ralph** I am awake.
**Anna** You can take your pills after your swim.
**Ralph** Yes, Anna.
**Anna** And have your walk after lunch.
**Ralph** Yes, Anna.

**Anna**  You won't need a siesta today. You've had that.

**Ralph**  Yes, Anna. No, Anna. Any more orders for the day?

**Anna**  It could have been Michael.

**Ralph**  What could?

**Anna**  On the phone.

**Ralph**  It wasn't.

**Anna**  You don't know that. If you'd stayed awake you would know.

**Ralph**  If he was going to call back, he's had plenty of time before now. He's not that busy. He hasn't. He doesn't intend to.

**Anna**  No, I suppose you're right.

**Ralph**  Thank you.

**Anna**  Perhaps if you were to phone yourself, he ——

**Ralph**  (*cutting in*) Anna, if he's determined to nurse his grudges, so be it. As far as I'm concerned, he's written out. Dropped from the diminishing cast list in my life for good. All right?

**Anna**  I don't know how you can be so nasty.

**Ralph**  Practice, my dear. A lifetime's endeavour. I've worked at it.

**Anna**  It's nothing to be proud of.

**Ralph**  I'm not going to grovel.

**Anna**  (*after a pause*) You remember about tomorrow?

**Ralph**  No. What?

**Anna**  It's my day for shopping in Rome.

**Ralph**  Oh, that.

**Anna**  I don't suppose you'd like to come with me?

**Ralph**  No. I'd like a day's peace and quiet. Blissful solitude.

**Anna**  (*getting up*) I think I'll go and change.

**Ralph**  Right.

*Anna moves towards the house, turns and looks back at Ralph*

**Anna**  If you never see Michael again, it's entirely your own doing.

**Ralph**  I know.

**Anna**  So long as you realize that.

**Ralph**  I do, Anna. I do.

**Anna**  You don't even know what guilt is, do you.

**Ralph**  Guilt is the most useless attribute ever wished upon the human race by fanatics with an open line to the Almighty. People who *know* what's right and wrong for everybody else.

**Anna**  For someone proud of his powers of reason, you do make silly, sweeping assertions.

**Ralph**  I know, but it's fun. Self-recrimination is like masturbation. A lonely occupation serving no practical end, gratifying only the wanker concerned.

**Anna**  In that case, you're not equipped to say why your Pontius Pilate lookalike should end his own life. You won't be able to make sense of it.
**Ralph**  Good God, woman, I don't have to commit murder to write about a murderer. There's a little bit of everything in all of us. I can identify, empathize ... oh, go away. Stop trying to teach me my trade.
**Anna**  That means I'm right. Whenever I'm right, you start blustering.

*Anna goes into the house*

*After a moment, Ralph raises his arm, looks at the "sting", touches it reflectively*

**Ralph**  (*to himself*) If he'd done it ... really done it ... how would it be, now?... like sleep, never waking up?... or something else? ... perception of some great truth? ... I wonder ...
**Anna**  (*off*) Ralph.
**Ralph**  Yes, Anna.
**Anna**  (*off*) I've laid out your swim things. Come and change.
**Ralph**  (*levering himself to his feet*) Yes, Anna.
**Anna**  (*off*) And don't forget to have your swim tomorrow, just because I shan't be here.
**Ralph**  No, Anna. (*To himself*) Perhaps it would be — peace. Sheer heavenly peace.
**Anna**  (*off*) Ralph.
**Ralph**  All right. All right.

*Black-out*

SCENE 2

*The same. Monday afternoon*

*The Lights come up on the courtyard/patio as before. No-one there*

*After a few moments, Ralph comes out of the house. He is wearing his hat, a towelling dressing-gown over swim trunks, sandals on his feet. A large towel (a bath sheet) is slung over his shoulder. He drops the towel on the couch, and sits on it, intending to remove his sandals, yawning a little*

*The light changes as a cloud obscures the sun. (No rolls of thunder though.) He looks up, studying the sky. Then, as he is about to bend again, he hears the sound of an approaching car. He looks at his watch, surprised, and stands up*

*The car stops, the engine is switched off*

*Anna appears, and comes through the gate, dressed for her shopping expedition*

**Ralph**  You're early.
**Anna**  Yes.
**Ralph**  Come back to make sure I'm obeying orders?
**Anna**  No. Are you? You've had your siesta?
**Ralph**  As instructed. I'm programmed. You've turned me into an automaton.
**Anna**  Rested? In a reasonably good humour?
**Ralph**  Hallo. That means trouble. What is it? A parking ticket?
**Anna**  No.
**Ralph**  You've banged the car.
**Anna**  Suppose I had.
**Ralph**  Anyone hurt?
**Anna**  No.
**Ralph**  (*anxiety showing*) You're all right?
**Anna**  Yes.
**Ralph**  (*a mental shrug*) Well, then. It's only a rented heap of metal.
**Anna**  My goodness, you're positively placid.
**Ralph**  Only don't expect me to deal with all the wretched paperwork.
**Anna**  There won't be any. I haven't had an accident.
**Ralph**  You said you had.
**Anna**  (*moving back to the gate*) No, I didn't. I said suppose. (*To someone out of sight*) You can come in now. It seems to be all right.
**Ralph**  Anna, you haven't picked up another of those penniless students you're convinced needs feeding and mothering.
**Anna**  No.

*Michael comes through the gate carrying a few articles of shopping (clearly not food). He pauses*

*Ralph, face set, stares at him. Michael's gaze in return is equally unpromising*

**Michael**  (*turning to Anna*) Shall I take these indoors?
**Anna**  Please. Just put them down somewhere.

*Michael takes the shopping into the house*

**Ralph**  (*not friendly*) You have been a busy little body.
**Anna**  Yes.

**Ralph**  Much too busy to shop for food, I notice.
**Anna**  I'm going now. (*She turns away to leave*)
**Ralph**  (*sternly*) Anna.

*Anna turns, defiant*

**Anna**  Yes?

*A long moment as they stare at each other*

  *Michael comes out of the house*

*Anna, seeing him, takes the opportunity to escape*

  Michael, I'm driving into the village. See you later.

  *Anna goes through the gate and out of sight*

*Ralph and Michael look at each other with wary unease. With feet planted
and arms at their sides they resemble a couple of boxers*

**Ralph**  (*about the sky and dull light*) Could be a storm coming up.
**Michael**  Yes.
**Ralph**  Might clear the air though. Usually does.
**Michael**  Not always.
**Ralph**  Been a bit oppressive lately, though, don't you think?
**Michael**  Yes.
**Ralph**  Well, suppose we sit down. Stop eyeing each other, like two boxers
  before the fight starts. Unfortunate simile. Ignore it. Besides you're not
  dressed for the part.

*Michael tries not to smile. There is the sound of the car starting and driving
away*

  (*After a pause*) Where did she track you down?
**Michael**  The studio canteen. Lunch break.
**Ralph**  Good God. How did she get in? Don't they have any security?
**Michael**  Supposed to be impregnable. No-one allowed in without a pass.
**Ralph**  Except Anna.
**Michael**  She talked them into giving her one.
**Ralph**  And then talked you into coming with her. What did she say?
**Michael**  She begged me to give you another chance. Apologized for your
  behaviour.

**Ralph** Did she indeed. You don't return phone calls, but Anna only has to turn up and say "please".

**Michael** It was "please, for me, Michael". Pleading. She was so insistent, I couldn't bring myself to hurt her by saying "no". That's the only reason I'm here.

**Ralph** Yes. I do things for that woman ... you're not alone, thinking "why am I doing this? I swore I wouldn't". It happens to me every day of my life. Was it inconvenient, getting away?

**Michael** Not really. Anna charmed the producer too. Well? What was so important?

*Ralph, now that he has the opportunity, is finding it hard to come to the point. He falls back on platitudes*

**Ralph** I only heard one car. Something wrong with yours?

**Michael** Debbie's using it.

**Ralph** Will she be collecting you?

**Michael** Anna said she'd drive me back.

**Ralph** Oh, well, that's fine. Fine. (*Pause*) I do miss not being able to light up, sometimes.

**Michael** Still?

**Ralph** Now and then. Difficult occasions. Work, for instance. When I get stuck. A cigarette was a trigger. Helped me concentrate. You never have. Or have you?

**Michael** No.

**Ralph** I suppose, your generation, it was drugs.

*A look from Michael*

Or maybe not.

**Michael** Most of us experimented. Soft drugs. It didn't do anything for me.

**Ralph** I know very little about you, I've realized. (*Pause*) There are things I have to say. Things you should know.

**Michael** I may have something to say to you, too.

**Ralph** Yes, I expect so. Well, unburden yourself first, if you like.

**Michael** I'd rather listen. I might decide not to.

**Ralph** The horizon recedes as we go through life. There's always tomorrow, next month, next year. The time comes when it stops receding. Mine has stopped. Quite soon, I shall die. Not a great event in your scheme of things. I haven't played much of a part in your life.

**Michael** Not much. Not really. No. Except ... (*He hesitates*)

**Ralph** I can't put that right. I'm not trying to. But I am your father. Even if I only ... acquired you ... and now ... I've lost the thread. Except what?

**Michael** The part you've played. Not the occasional duty visitor ...

**Ralph** The man who sent cheques. I've gathered that.

**Michael** What you were. The film-maker. That novel. What you achieved. That mattered. That it was my father who'd done all that.

**Ralph** "Success" so-called? Making money?

**Michael** Only partly. Mostly, the style, the insights. What you did was original and truthful and good.

**Ralph** My word, what a reference for my tombstone.

**Michael** But none of that was in the occasional visitor. It belonged to someone I didn't know at all. Still, he was my father. It provided ... something to aim at. That's the "except".

**Ralph** Outdo your old man. Put him in the shade.

**Michael** I doubt it. I'm not that good.

**Ralph** Talent is something you're born with. Where mine came from, God knows. My father was a bricklayer. My mother worked in a sweet shop before they married. I haunted the public library. Read everything, anything, all the time. That library was my university.

**Michael** Not like me, you mean, who had it easy. Is that it?

**Ralph** I wasn't bragging. The self-educated man can be subject to certain failings.

**Michael** Such as?

**Ralph** Arrogance, pride, self-assertion. I do know, Michael.

**Michael** You've hidden it well, in that case.

**Ralph** Talent requires the manure of hard work or it neither grows nor flourishes. But I was always a worker. Stress was no problem, it gave me a lift. Rather like you, I fancy.

**Michael** I don't mind working under pressure, no. Quite enjoy it as a matter of fact.

**Ralph** So do I. Along with some talent and much stamina, I had a facility. I could work fast. Make it look easy.

**Michael** Nothing wrong with that.

**Ralph** Facility. Believe me, facility is a harlot in disguise. When I look back over my life, the truth is, too often I've trimmed, I've compromised, I have not used to the full those talents I was given.

**Michael** Does anyone?

**Ralph** They can try. Harder than I have. I can't go back and do it all over again. Except, perhaps through you.

**Michael** I can only find my own way.

**Ralph** Yes, of course ...

**Michael** I can't have ... your regrets ... your wishes ... imposed on me.

**Ralph** There are better models for a young writer than your father. Talent is like money. It's easily squandered.

**Michael** Isn't that rather a facile thing to say when you've had plenty of both?

**Ralph** Not always. No-one gave me any money. I had to earn it.

**Michael** Then you remember what it's like.

**Ralph** You won't let me help you ...

**Michael** No. It has to be ... without you.

**Ralph** Well, perhaps one day, when the harlot Facility smiles at you, you'll recall this conversation.

**Michael** Just now, I'd embrace the bitch if she'd offer me a couple of scripts.

**Ralph** Your contract up soon?

**Michael** Yes.

**Ralph** Would you do something for me?

**Michael** Tell me what, and I'll tell you.

**Ralph** Read my current work in progress.

**Michael** Pontius Pilate?

**Ralph** If you can bear to.

**Michael** Now?

**Ralph** It's not complete. Thirty or forty pages, that's all.

**Michael** Well, if you like ...

**Ralph** (*pointing to his work room*) It's in there. Print it out. You know how to work those things, I'm sure.

*Puzzled, Michael goes into the house*

*After a few moments, there is the sound of the printer at work*

*Michael appears and stands looking at Ralph*

*The sound of the printer continues. The sky begins to lighten, the light improves*

**Michael** How soon is "quite soon"?

**Ralph** (*turning*) What? Oh, my demise, you mean. Not long.

**Michael** Anna said the operation was a success.

**Ralph** There was something else, yes. Some young, smart-arse doctor thought he'd detected something. A body scan confirmed it.

**Michael** Isn't there something they can do? Another operation? Anything?

**Ralph** Nothing. Contrary to popular myth, the miracles of modern medicine can neither confer permanent good health, nor prolong life indefinitely.

**Michael** Does Anna know?

**Ralph** No.

**Michael** Don't you think you should tell her?

**Ralph** (*shaking his head*) It would cause her needless unhappiness. Much better if it just happens, all over quickly. Kinder, to her.

**Michael** Is that likely?

**Ralph** It could well happen suddenly, yes.

*Sunlight penetrates on to the courtyard/patio. The sound of the printer stops*

Ready for you. I think the storm could be passing us by.
**Michael** Yes.

*Ralph sits down on the couch. He pulls his hat over his eyes*

**Ralph** I think I shall have a doze.

   *Michael looks at him for a moment then goes into the house. He closes the
   door as he goes in*

*There is silence for a few moments*

   *The Visitor appears at the gate, carrying his bag*

**Visitor** (*a polite smile*) Good-afternoon, sir.
**Ralph** (*bewildered*) What the hell ...

*Ralph pushes his hat back and stands up*

**Visitor** I happened to be nearby. (*Indicating*) No car outside. I supposed you
   might be alone.
**Ralph** You've got a bloody nerve. You cheat me, you walk off with my
   money ... you — you charlatan ...
**Visitor** I did suggest you took time to reflect. That I should call again in a
   day or so.
**Ralph** That's why you're here?
**Visitor** Instant on-the-spot decisions, I'm wary, sir. Very wary. When we're
   dealing with something so very final.
**Ralph** What was it? Valium?
**Visitor** Just a little something to induce sleep. Are you sorry you woke up?
**Ralph** (*after a pause*) No.
**Visitor** I suspected we might have a change of heart.
**Ralph** I didn't say that.

*The Visitor looks at Ralph, enquiringly*

**Visitor** No?
**Ralph** Someone called unexpectedly. Someone I'd given up hope of seeing
   again.

**Visitor** Well, then, my deception evidently served a good purpose.

**Ralph** Yes, it did.

**Visitor** Good.

**Ralph** May I ask you something?

**Visitor** Of course.

**Ralph** My condition ... I'd like to know ... truthfully ... how it would be ... without your help ...

**Visitor** I'd imagine that has been explained to you.

**Ralph** Not really. I think they were trying to be kind, reassuring, make it sound bearable.

**Visitor** Anything can be borne. And it may be worthwhile doing so. That's a matter for the individual.

**Ralph** They gave me ... well, that was a while ago ... from now, perhaps six months. About. They said they couldn't be precise.

**Visitor** No-one can. Any pain yet?

**Ralph** Spasms. Quite trying but — not too bad. It doesn't last. Later, I suppose, it will.

**Visitor** Pain can be controlled.

**Ralph** What does that mean? Drugged senseless day and night?

**Visitor** (*shaking his head*) Drugs can be given in small, continuous doses, thus avoiding drowsiness, but controlling even intense pain.

**Ralph** (*a doubtful look*) H'm. Yes. Well ... (*Changing tack*) Loss of weight? Increasing weakness?

**Visitor** Probably.

**Ralph** Bedridden?

**Visitor** Excellent nursing would be provided.

**Ralph** My wife was a nurse. Carried on doing voluntary work until quite recently.

**Visitor** Well, in that case ...

**Ralph** No. Transfer my pain, my helplessness on to her? No. I won't do that.

**Visitor** Is that a decision for you? Should it not be hers?

**Ralph** We used to have a dog. It got old and sick. The vet said he could keep it alive for a while, but it would be kinder not to. She cried when it was put down. But that was better than watching the poor beast suffer. Better for her.

**Visitor** How long had you had your dog?

**Ralph** Fourteen years.

**Visitor** And your wife?

**Ralph** We shan't make our twenty-fifth anniversary.

**Visitor** So you were by no means a young man when you married her.

**Ralph** No.

**Visitor** Previously?

**Ralph** Marriage? No. There were women, of course. Always someone I found attractive at the time.

**Visitor** Physically attractive.

**Ralph** Well, yes, although some of them happened to be very clever and talented as well.

**Visitor** But?

**Ralph** In the end, it was always unsatisfactory.

**Visitor** A little like the imaginary character in your novel, middle aged, weary of loveless affairs.

**Ralph** (*drily*) Do you know, that never occurred to me.

**Visitor** But your wife is different in some way to all the others.

**Ralph** Oh, yes.

**Visitor** How?

**Ralph** (*after a pause*) Anna is my best friend.

**Visitor** Well, a dog may be a man's best friend too, but I would suggest that her relationship with you is probably rather different. You would be depriving her of a last few months together. Time. A chance to say things perhaps. To express feelings. The survivor can often draw great comfort and strength from those last weeks and months.

**Ralph** You're not much of a salesman, are you.

**Visitor** Sometimes, my prospects have not considered every aspect.

**Ralph** I understand what you're saying. But I see ... her face ... as she watches me ... cares for me ... while I ... decline, decay ... become ... a pitiful object ... instead of more or less the man she married, for good or ill. I see the humiliation my own father suffered during his last months on this earth, helpless, incontinent, but aware. Saying: "Let me die, let me die". But death would not come. Do you understand me?

**Visitor** Oh yes. You are not the first to express similar sentiments.

**Ralph** Will you oblige me?

**Visitor** Is that truly your wish?

**Ralph** You've made it less simple than I thought ... but ... yes.

*The Visitor opens his bag*

**Visitor** Now?

**Ralph** (*quickly*) No.

*A look from the Visitor*

There's someone here. (*He indicates the house*) My son.

**Visitor** Ah. The someone you feared you would never see again.

**Ralph** A last chance to make my peace with him — so, another time. When I'm ready.

**Visitor** Of course.

*The Visitor eyes Ralph thoughtfully*

Before I go, may I ask *you* something?

**Ralph** Isn't the dissection over? I thought you'd taken me apart pretty comprehensively.

**Visitor** Mere curiosity this time. I'm always interested in a man's beginnings.

**Ralph** As well as his ending.

**Visitor** My path was almost foreordained; to follow my father's footsteps. Yours, I take it, was less direct.

**Ralph** One forgets, but yes, I suppose so. I won a scholarship to a grammar school, left at sixteen, as most boys did in those days. I became a junior clerk in an insurance office. My parents were delighted. A safe job for life. The fruits of all their sacrifices. I loathed it, the endless hours of tedium. My escape was the cinema. That was where I came alive. (*He looks at the Visitor*) I got a job as a runner at Pinewood Studios. What the Americans call a gopher. Go fer this, go fer that.

**Visitor** Your parents, how did they feel about this?

**Ralph** Hurt, poor souls. Hurt and bewildered. They'd never known security, I'd thrown it away — and for less money. After a while, I got myself into the cutting room, began editing, started writing. The path straightened out after that.

**Visitor** And your parents realized you'd done the right thing.

**Ralph** I think they only really accepted that when I was able to buy a decent house for them.

*The Visitor nods and takes Ralph's small bag from his bag and puts it down*

**Visitor** Illuminating. Thank you. I shall leave this with you.

**Ralph** No, no, keep it.

**Visitor** You may return it to me. Should we meet again.

**Ralph** I shan't change my mind.

**Visitor** Then we shall. Until then, I shall wish you good-day.

**Ralph** I'll be in touch.

*The Visitor nods, and leaves*

*After a few moments, Michael comes out of the house. He carries a sheaf of A4 typescript, say forty pages. Any visible are laid out as for a film script*

**Michael** Has he gone?

**Ralph** Who?

**Michael** I thought there was someone here.

**Ralph** Oh, yes. Some fool selling life insurance. I got rid of him. (*About the typescript*) Well?

*Michael moves about as they talk: a sign of unease*

**Michael** It's very good. I like it.

**Ralph** (*gratified*) Truly?

**Michael** The best thing you've ever done.

**Ralph** You really think so?

**Michael** Oh, yes. Can't wait to see the rest. The characters, everything. Marvellous.

**Ralph** Michael, you are an abject liar. It's terrible. Worse than any of that crap you're engaged in.

**Michael** (*lamely*) It's not that bad.

**Ralph** Stop looking shifty and sit down.

*Michael sits near Ralph*

Now be honest.

**Michael** Well, it needs a bit more work ...

**Ralph** It needs a match put to it.

**Michael** No, really, some of the early scenes, especially the visual stuff ... they're fine.

**Ralph** Dressed up with an old dog's tricks. Sleight of hand. Candy floss.

**Michael** (*lamely*) It's still a very good idea.

**Ralph** (*touching his head*) It's there. Inside. The concept. That half formed vision. I can still talk a good movie, but I can't do it any more. I've lost it. The facility, much less any quality. It's gone.

**Michael** Perhaps the subject wasn't right for you.

**Ralph** (*pointing to the typescript*) I wanted to do that. Really wanted to. For it to be good. The one thing, I could say "worth a lifetime's work to write that". My masterwork, as Anna insists on calling it. Illusions. An old man's fantasies.

**Michael** I'm sorry.

**Ralph** Don't be. I know the truth. I pissed away whatever talent I had in the days when the offers poured in.

*Michael stands*

**Michael** (*with some resentment*) Why ask me to read it? You must have known ... I'd want it to be good. What was it? Some sort of test?

**Ralph** No. You have a kindness I lack. I knew what you'd say. I'm a working animal. Take away the work, and I scarcely exist. Until now, I've kept going. Trying to do this. Set up that. Blaming anyone but myself when it didn't happen. (*Pointing at the typescript*) That told me. Now I know.

**Michael** If you knew, you didn't need anyone else's opinion, least of all mine. I'd rather not have known.

**Ralph** When you can make choices, take more care of your talent than I did. I've finished.

**Michael** (*after a pause*) There's something I suppose I should tell you.

**Ralph** Go ahead.

**Michael** Debbie's pregnant.

**Ralph** What?

**Michael** Pregnant.

**Ralph** Yours?

**Michael** (*a look*) Yes.

**Ralph** It didn't show. Early days.

**Michael** Fairly.

**Ralph** No problem then. Do you need help? If so ——

**Michael** No.

**Ralph** A good man can be expensive. Let me. I will, gladly.

**Michael** Forget I mentioned it. I should have known which way your mind would turn. Bring out your bloody cheque book.

**Ralph** Now what's wrong?

**Michael** She'll have it. She wants it.

**Ralph** Oh. Do you?

**Michael** Yes. Believe it or not. Yes.

**Ralph** You're turning me into a bloody grandfather?

**Michael** Looks like it.

**Ralph** (*a perverse change of mood*) A grandchild?

**Michael** Yes.

**Ralph** Well, I'm damned.

**Michael** Sorry, but there it is.

**Ralph** A grandchild. (*He has a thought*) I'll have to change my will. Include him. Or her.

**Michael** You don't have to do that. That's not why I told you.

**Ralph** No, no, must leave the little bastard something.

**Michael** As it happens, he, or she, won't be.

**Ralph** Be what?

**Michael** A bastard. We're getting married.

**Ralph** Whose idea is that?

**Michael** Both of us. We intended to, anyway. A bit sooner now, that's all.

**Ralph** When?

**Michael** Early next month.

**Ralph**  Am I invited? No, I don't suppose she'd have me.

**Michael**  You didn't impress her much. She thinks you're a pig.

**Ralph**  I know. I am a pig. I know. (*Almost humble*) Will you bring her to see me? Please? I'll behave. Truly.

**Michael**  She won't make it easy for you. She can dish it out, if she's provoked.

**Ralph**  Yes, I did kind of realize that. Try and persuade her, won't you.

**Michael**  If I can.

**Ralph**  Tell her she can have as many free shies at the old coconut as she likes. I'll be meek and mild as mother's milk. I'll grovel.

**Michael**  You really are a perverse old bugger.

**Ralph**  What have I said now?

**Michael**  That you'd be pleased about it was the last thing I expected.

**Ralph**  No, well, I wouldn't have predicted that either. But now it's happened, I am. My "immortality" in that girl's womb. A selfish reaction, I know, but good news has been a bit thin on the ground lately.

**Michael**  It's all right. Nice to have approval about something for a change.

**Ralph**  When is it due? This child?

**Michael**  About six months.

**Ralph**  Six months. I wonder ... (*His voice dies away*)

**Michael**  What?

**Ralph**  It would be good to see my grandchild, before I depart this life. I'd like that.

**Michael**  So would I.

**Ralph**  Why not? Perhaps I could ... it's possible ...

**Michael**  You said it could be — any time.

**Ralph**  Yes, I know, but — perhaps he was right ——

**Michael**  Who?

**Ralph**  (*ignoring the question; inward reflection*) — something to hang on for ... perhaps I was thinking about myself as usual ... not really considering Anna ... (*He looks at Michael*) They said I had up to six months from now. But they don't know everything, these quacks. Perhaps I can fool the bastards. You never know ... a remission ... or I might even beat it ...

*There is the sound of a car approaching, then coming to a stop*

(*Pointing to the typescript*) Michael, I don't want her to see that.

**Michael**  (*picking up the typescript*) In your study?

*The sound of a car door opening and slamming closed*

**Ralph**  Hide it somewhere, anywhere. (*He registers the small bag*) And this too. (*He picks up the bag*)

**Michael** (*taking the bag*) OK.

*Michael takes the articles into the house*

*Ralph sits in a chair near the table. He feigns sleep, his hat over his eyes*

*After a few moments Anna comes through the gate, carrying food shopping*

*Anna, expecting to see Michael, stops, and looks round*

**Anna**  Ralph?

*Ralph "wakes up"*

**Ralph**  Oh, hallo. (*He yawns and stretches*) You've been quick.
**Anna**  No, I haven't.
**Ralph**  Really? What time is it?
**Anna**  Where's Michael, may I ask?
**Ralph**  Michael?
**Anna**  Your son.
**Ralph**  (*looking round the courtyard/patio*) Well, I don't see him here, do you?
**Anna**  All right. What happened?
**Ralph**  Nothing happened.
**Anna**  So. You've done it again. I despair. I really do despair.
**Ralph**  Despair of what?
**Anna**  You. You and your bad temper.
**Ralph**  I'm not in a bad temper. I've had a very pleasant afternoon.
**Anna**  You said something to upset him. You must have done.
**Ralph**  Nonsense. I was sweetness and light itself.
**Anna**  Then why isn't he still here?

*Ralph shrugs*

And how was he supposed to get back to Rome? Didn't you think about that?
**Ralph**  It didn't cross my mind to be honest.
**Anna**  Oh, really!
**Ralph**  You didn't pass him then.
**Anna**  No, of course not, or I'd have stopped.
**Ralph**  Oh, yes. So you would.
**Anna**  I'm very angry with you, Ralph. I've never been so angry with you before in the whole of my life.

**Ralph** I think you're exaggerating. I'm sure you have, many times.
**Anna** Oh. Sometimes, I could ... oh!

*Michael wanders out of the house*

*Anna sees him*

**Michael** Hallo. You've been quick.
**Anna** Michael.
**Michael** Shopping all done?
**Anna** You're here.
**Michael** Well, yes. Shouldn't I be?

*Anna turns and glares at Ralph who is convulsed with suppressed laughter*

**Anna** You're an evil old man, and I hate you.
**Michael** What's he done?
**Ralph** (*hugging himself in delight, still laughing*) You will sit up and beg for
   it, Anna ... oh ... I can't help it ... I just can't resist it ...
**Michael** (*looking from one to the other*) Is this a private joke?
**Anna** Private, but not funny.

*Ralph is still laughing*

   That loathsome person thinks it is, of course. I don't like being laughed at,
   Ralph. (*She brushes past Michael*) Excuse me. (*To Ralph as she goes*)
   You've done that once too often.

*Anna goes into the house with her shopping*

*Michael watches her go, and then looks at Ralph*

**Ralph** Nothing to worry about. She subsides as fast as she flares up. Where
   did you put it?
**Michael** Top shelf in the tall cupboard. The bag too.
**Ralph** I'll chuck it out sometime when madam isn't around. Wipe the disk.
   Forget it.
**Michael** In a way, you know, it's there. What you were after.
**Ralph** Except it isn't.
**Michael** I think it could be made to work.
**Ralph** Do you? How? No, don't tell me. Can't stand salvage jobs. Never
   could.
**Michael** Wouldn't do any harm to look at it again, before you decide.

**Ralph** I don't know ... I'll think about it ... Better still, have a go at it yourself.

**Michael** (*after a pause*) I took you at your word.

**Ralph** Eh? What word?

**Michael** Phoned Debbie. She's coming to pick me up.

**Ralph** Oh. How was she? On the cool side?

**Michael** Closer to icy. If you'd rather, I'll call back and cancel.

**Ralph** No. Get it over with. Anna's going to adore this. You'll witness unadulterated smug satisfaction. She's always recommending a diet of humble pie. Hallo!

*Anna comes out of the house*

Hallo, my dear.

**Anna** (*to Michael; pointedly ignoring Ralph*) Could you stay for dinner, Michael?

**Ralph** What are we having?

**Anna** Michael?

**Michael** The thing is, Debbie's collecting me, later.

**Anna** And she won't want to stay and be insulted again. No, of course.

**Michael** (*about Ralph*) In fact, it's his idea. He wants to see her.

**Ralph** It's grovel grovel time. My Uriah Heep impersonation. Anna's revenge. You'll love it.

**Anna** (*to Michael*) She's more than welcome, if she can bear to sit at the same table with this disagreeable individual.

**Ralph** I shall be charming and wonderful, as always.

**Michael** (*to Anna*) Then we will. If there's enough.

**Anna** Plenty. That's settled then. What a nice surprise.

**Ralph** Say thank you, Ralph, for being a good boy.

*Finally, Anna directs an, as yet, unforgiving gaze at Ralph*

**Anna** (*cool*) Facetiousness in a man of your years smacks of second childhood.

**Ralph** Well, the first one was a bit brief. I'm making up for it.

**Anna** You don't propose to sit down to dinner like that, I hope.

*Ralph stands up at once*

**Ralph** I shall go and change immediately. At once.

*Anna crosses, picks up Ralph's dry towel and holds it to her cheek*

**Anna** No, you won't. You haven't had your swim. And don't pretend you have. I can tell.

*Anna throws the towel at Ralph, who catches it*

Now. In the pool.
**Ralph** Yes, Matron. Understood, Matron.

*Ralph moves towards the side of the pool, takes off his wrist-watch, and puts it in his dressing-gown pocket*

**Anna** And use the steps. Don't hurl yourself off the diving board like an old walrus.
**Ralph** I wish you'd hold your breath for about twenty-five minutes.
**Anna** (*to Michael*) He decided he could still dive in the other day, and he can't. He looked ridiculous.

*Ralph pauses, just before he goes out of sight*

**Ralph** Michael, you'd better tell her your bad news.

*Ralph moves on, out of sight. When Ralph speaks, off, although his voice is not distressed, it is the breathy tone of a man engaged in physical exercise*

**Anna** Bad news? Michael ...
**Ralph** (*off*) Terrible. The worst.
**Anna** (*to Michael*) What bad news?
**Michael** Debbie's pregnant. We're getting married. All good.
**Anna** I see. (*A glance at the pool*) But he thinks not.
**Michael** No. He's all in favour. Much enamoured by the idea of a grandchild.
**Anna** (*her feelings showing*) Is he indeed. Well. (*But a smile for Michael*) And you're happy about it?
**Michael** Very. Debbie too.
**Anna** Then it is the best of news.

*A quick congratulatory embrace*

Wonderful. Congratulations.
**Michael** Thank you.
**Anna** Much enamoured ... he will make up to Debbie, so that she will let him see the baby. Is that it?
**Michael** Along those lines, I think.

**Anna**  A grandchild is all right, it seems.
**Michael**  (*a close look at Anna*) Is something wrong, Anna?

*Anna smiles, touches his arm in a gesture of reassurance*

**Anna**  No, no. He's so contradictory, he still takes me by surprise, that's all.
**Michael**  I told him he was perverse.
**Anna**  Perverse is better. Perverse is right.
**Ralph**  (*off*) Has he broken it to you yet?
**Anna**  Yes, I've heard all about it. (*Rather louder than before*) Well, this must
be a celebration. We should open a bottle of champagne. No, perhaps with
dinner.
**Ralph**  (*off*) It's not rationed. Now, and with dinner.

*Anna moves and looks out at Ralph*

**Anna**  Don't tire yourself.
**Ralph**  (*off*) I'm all right. Feel good. Enjoying it.
**Anna**  Well, slow down, for goodness' sake. You'll never break any speed
records with that silly doggypaddle.
**Ralph**  (*off*) It is not a doggypaddle. (*Pause*) It's a racing breast stroke.

*Anna turns away towards Michael. Body bent forward, head held back, she
takes a few steps forward, miming Ralph's stroke*

**Anna**  He swims like a rheumatic dog. It's a doggypaddle. (*She straightens
up*) Would you like a glass of champagne now? Or should we wait for
Debbie.
**Michael**  Now sounds good to me. (*He sits*)
**Ralph**  (*off*) Where's the champagne?

*Anna returns to the pool and looks out at Ralph*

**Anna**  You're not allowed any.
**Ralph**  (*off*) Oh, come on. It's an occasion.
**Anna**  Well, perhaps one small glass. And I do mean one.
**Ralph**  (*off*) Right. That's got me out.

*There are sounds off indicating Ralph is leaving the pool*

**Anna**  And make sure you dry yourself properly.
**Ralph**  (*off*) All right, Matron. All right.

*Anna turns away from the pool*

**Michael**  Can I do anything to help?
**Anna**  I'll bring everything. You open the bottle.
**Michael**  Right.
**Anna**  (*quietly*) I am truly pleased for you, Michael.
**Michael**  I know.
**Anna**  (*quietly*) If I could have had children — I'd have liked that very much ... for a moment, I expect I was jealous ... please forgive me.
**Michael**  Don't be silly.
**Anna**  Well, I was being silly. And I'm sorry. (*Louder, towards Ralph*) Champagne on the way. Time to celebrate.

*Anna hurries into the house*

**Michael**  (*after a pause, to Ralph, off*) How much longer will you be staying in Italy?

*Longish pause*

*Ralph appears. He has dried himself and donned his bathrobe, and is trailing his towel*

**Ralph**  (*breathlessly, in distress, with difficulty*) Michael ... Michael ...
**Michael**  (*alarmed*) What is it? What's wrong?

*As he speaks, Michael is on his feet, and moving quickly to meet Ralph who is barely able to move. His face is ashen, covered in cold sweat. His skin would be cold to the touch. Michael supports Ralph and leads him to a chair*

What's happened?
**Ralph**  Can't breathe ... my heart ...

*Michael assists Ralph on to the chair*

**Michael**  (*calling urgently*) Anna. Anna. Here. Quickly.
**Ralph**  Just happened ... no warning ...

*Anna hurries from the house, takes in the situation at a glance. From here on, she is in command, professional and cool*

**Michael**  It's his heart.

*Michael moves aside. Anna bends over Ralph and touches his skin*

**Ralph**  Heart racing ... won't stop ... can't breathe ...
**Anna**  Don't talk. Try and relax.

*Anna stands erect*

(*To Michael*) There's a doctor in the village. I'll phone. You stay with him.

*Anna hurries into the house*

*Michael returns to the chair and crouches beside it*

**Ralph**  Michael ...
**Michael**  I'm here.
**Ralph**  Tell Anna ...
**Michael**  You mustn't talk.
**Ralph**  Listen ... tell her ... with my will ... it's there ... she'll see ...
**Michael**  I'll tell her.
**Ralph**  Tell Anna ... with the will ...
**Michael**  I'll tell her, now that's enough. The doctor'll be here soon.

*There is a pause, and then Ralph loops his arms limply round Michael's neck and draws him into a gentle embrace*

**Ralph**  With ... will ...
**Michael**  Ssh. You mustn't.

*And Ralph's arms fall from around Michael's neck. His body is limp. His lower jaw has dropped slightly*

(*Softly; appalled*) Ralph. Ralph.

*Anna hurries from the house*

**Anna**  (*entering*) The ambulance is on its way.
**Michael**  (*standing up*) I think it's too late, Anna.

*Anna establishes that Ralph has ceased breathing. During the ensuing sequence, she is urgent but controlled*

**Anna**  Help me lift him on to the ground.
**Michael**  What?

**Anna** We have to get him breathing again. We need a hard surface. Quickly.

*During the following, they lift Ralph from the chair and place him on the ground. He is placed so that, when Michael kneels and bends over him, his body mostly shields Ralph from us*

He needs mouth to mouth and heart massage. Do you know what to do?
**Michael** No. Tell me.

*Michael kneels down beside Ralph. Anna places his hands on Ralph's chest*

**Anna** When I say, you press down hard five times, here. Do you understand?

*Michael nods. Anna breathes into Ralph's mouth*

Now.

*Michael presses down five times*

Good. Again.

*Anna breathes into Ralph's mouth. Michael presses down five times*

Again.

*Anna breathes into Ralph's mouth. And as Michael presses down the Lights fade to Black-out*

SCENE 3

*The same. Evening*

*The sky is not completely dark, but night is falling. The lights in the house are on, as are the lights on the courtyard/patio. The sun umbrella is down (if used)*

*Debbie is sitting in a chair beside the table. Michael drifts about restlessly*

**Michael** (*after a pause*) If I'd been alone with him, he'd be dead. She saved his life.
**Debbie** You helped.
**Michael** (*a shaky smile*) Not something I'd care to do again. Terrifying.
**Debbie** It worked.

**Michael** She said, she probably couldn't have done it, on her own. He still looked ghastly, his face grey ... but at least he was breathing ... just about ...

**Debbie** He's in good hands now. You did all you could.

**Michael** He was pleased about us, the baby, really pleased.

**Debbie** I know.

**Michael** Oh, yes. I told you.

**Debbie** Yes.

**Michael** Sorry.

**Debbie** It's all right.

**Michael** Sort of delayed reaction. Can't quite take it in. (*He looks at his watch*) She said she'd ring.

**Debbie** He'll be in intensive care. There may be nothing to say yet.

**Michael** I think I'll phone the hospital.

*Michael begins to move towards the house. Debbie hears the sound of Anna's car approaching. She stands up*

**Debbie** Michael.

*Michael pauses and listens. A flash of swivelling headlights as the car comes to a stop. The headlights and engine are switched off. The car door closes*

*Anna appears and comes through the gate. She registers Debbie's presence*

**Anna** (*rather vaguely*) Debbie. Of course, you were coming. I'd forgotten. I'm sorry.

**Debbie** How is he?

**Anna** He was dead on arrival.

*There is a shocked moment as Michael and Debbie take this in. Anna seems calm, no tears. Debbie moves to Anna and holds her*

**Debbie** Oh, Anna, how you must feel. I'm so sorry.

*Anna pats Debbie's back as if she were consoling Debbie*

**Anna** Thank you, my dear. Thank you.

*Anna is looking across at Michael as she moves away from Debbie*

And thank you, Michael, for helping me. I know how hard it must have been for you.

**Michael** He died in the ambulance? I thought they carried all sorts of equipment.

**Anna** They did everything possible. It wasn't a great surprise. The prognosis was never good, once he'd stopped breathing. But it was worth trying. We had to try.

**Debbie** Would you like something, Anna? Coffee, a drink, I don't know, anything ...

**Anna** I don't think so, thank you. They were very kind at the hospital, looked after me until I felt able to drive back. It's strange, I still feel his presence. As if he were somewhere — just out of sight.

*Anna looks at Michael and Debbie*

I'm not silly. I always knew I'd probably be left alone one day. I did hope we might have another five or ten years but ... that wasn't to be.

**Debbie** Say no if you'd rather, but would you like me to come and stay with you? For a few days anyway?

**Anna** You're very kind, Debbie, but I shall be fine, you know. There's always so much to see to after a death. I'd like him buried back home, so that I can have a grave to visit. All that kind of thing.

**Michael** I'd be glad to help in any way I can, Anna. Phone calls, arrangements, anything.

**Anna** Oh, I know how busy you are, Michael. I wouldn't wish to impose.

**Michael** It's not an imposition. I think I should. He was my father.

**Anna** Then yes. I'd appreciate it. Thank you. Both of you.

**Michael** Don't keep saying thank you, Anna. You've nothing to thank us for.

**Anna** You're here, Michael. And that helps. (*Pause*) He could be something of an old devil as you well know. But sometimes, not. I shall miss him dreadfully.

**Michael** He asked me to tell you there was something for you with his will.

**Anna** Did he? What?

**Michael** I don't know, but it must have seemed important to him. It was the last thing he said.

**Anna** Well, I suppose I should find out what it is.

*Anna moves towards the house then pauses*

I hope there'll be no need for a post mortem. I wouldn't like to think of his poor body being cut about, even though I know he's left it. I wouldn't like that.

*Anna goes into the house*

**Debbie** (*quietly*) She's very strong, but she's not as composed as she seems.

**Michael** Would she really rather be left alone, do you think?

**Debbie** (*a negative*) She needs to talk about him. You're the best one. You're his son.

**Michael** All my life, I hardly knew him. This afternoon, for an hour, I began to know him. Enough to think, "Yes, we could get on. You and me. I think I do like you after all." Under that indifferent, protective hard shell of his, he did care in his own strange way. It seemed like — a beginning. I feel I've ... lost more than I expected.

*Debbie moves to Michael, holds him in an embrace, for a few moments*

**Debbie** You came to see him. I expect that hour mattered to him too. You gave him that.

**Michael** (*as they separate*) It doesn't seem enough.

**Debbie** It's all there was time for.

*Anna comes out of the house. She carries a will, and an envelope on which is printed "Anna"*

**Anna** (*handing the will to Michael*) You may as well look at his will some time, Michael. I know you're a beneficiary. He didn't tell me how much.

**Michael** I didn't expect anything.

**Anna** Well, that was what he wanted. (*A glance to include Debbie*) Now, more than ever, I'm sure. And I think he made you his Literary Executor. I expect you'll want to look through all his papers, his unfinished work, just in case ... Well, I'll leave all that to you.

*Michael holds the will uncertainly, while Anna opens the envelope, takes out a letter several pages long, and puts on her glasses*

(*Reading aloud*) "You will be reading this very soon ..." (*She stops reading and looks up*) It's dated last Saturday. As if he knew. How could he?

**Michael** Anna, he didn't tell you, but he had a ... (*He breaks off*)

**Anna** A what?

**Michael** (*changing his mind*) A premonition. He mentioned it to me.

**Anna** Oh.

*Anna's eyes return to the letter, skims through some, then pauses*

(*Reading aloud*) "I am told that I take but do not give, and so it must seem. I have always found it difficult to display my true feelings. It is a fault in me. But the truth is that you are the only woman I have truly loved. Every moment since the day we met, through our life together, I have loved you always, and I want you to ..." (*She stops reading, folds the letter and puts it back inside the envelope*) Oh, I'll read the rest later. It was very thoughtful of him to leave this, but I know all that. He didn't have to tell me. I always knew.

CURTAIN

# FURNITURE AND PROPERTY LIST

## ACT I
### Scene 1

| | |
|---|---|
| *On stage*: | Climbing plants, shrubs in pots, potted plants<br>Garden table<br>3 garden chairs<br>Couch<br>Sun umbrella (up), or olive tree<br>Portable radio<br>Book (for **Anna**)<br>Venetian blinds at windows (closed) |
| *Off stage*: | Tray containing 4 glasses of iced, fruit-decorated drinks, jug for refilling (**Anna**) |
| *Personal*: | **Anna**: reading spectacles, wrist-watch<br>**Michael**: wrist-watch<br>**Ralph**: wrist-watch |

### Scene 2

| | |
|---|---|
| *Strike*: | Tray, 4 glasses, jug, portable radio, book |
| *Re-set*: | Sun umbrella down |
| *Set*: | Tea cup on table |

### Scene 3

| | |
|---|---|
| *Strike*: | Tea cup from table |
| *Set*: | Fat envelope containing banknotes on table<br>Small leather bag containing banknotes in plant pot |
| *Re-set*: | Sun umbrella up |
| *Off stage*: | Doctor-type bag containing hypodermic syringe, ampoule, medical swab (**Visitor**) |
| *Personal*: | **Ralph**: typed letter in pocket |

63

ACT II
Scene 1

*On stage*:    As before

*Off stage*:   Cotton wool, small bottle (**Anna**)

*Personal*:    **Anna**: handbag

Scene 2

*On stage*:    As before

*Off stage*:   Large towel (**Ralph**)
               Few articles of shopping (**Michael**)
               Sheaf of A4 typescript (**Michael**)
               Food shopping (**Anna**)

Scene 3

*Strike*:      Large towel

*Re-set*:      Sun umbrella down

*Off stage*:   Will, envelope containing letter several pages long (**Anna**)

# LIGHTING PLOT

Practical fittings required: 2 lamps
Exterior. The same scene throughout

ACT I, SCENE 1. Midsummer afternoon

*To open*: Full sunshine

*Cue* 1      **Ralph** is left sitting      (Page 20)
          *Black-out*

ACT I, SCENE 2. Midsummer evening

*To open*: General night effect with faint moonlight on house, practicals on with covering spots

*Cue* 2      **Ralph**: "Oh, Anna ... Anna ..."      (Page 25)
          *Black-out*

ACT I, SCENE 3. Midsummer morning

*To open*: Bright sunshine

*Cue* 3      The **Visitor** moves out of sight      (Page 32)
          *Fade to black-out*

ACT II, SCENE 1. Midsummer morning

*To open*: Hot late morning sunshine

*Cue* 4      **Ralph**: "All right. All right."      (Page 37)
          *Black-out*

ACT II, SCENE 2. Midsummer afternoon

*To open*:  Bright sunshine

| *Cue* 5 | **Ralph** sits on the couch | (Page 37) |
| | *Sunshine dimmed, lighting becomes dull* | |

| *Cue* 6 | **Michael** stands looking at **Ralph** | (Page 42) |
| | *Lighting brightens gradually* | |

| *Cue* 7 | **Ralph**: "It could well happen suddenly, yes." | (Page 43) |
| | *Bright sunshine* | |

| *Cue* 8 | **Michael** presses down (3rd time) | (Page 57) |
| | *Fade to black-out* | |

ACT II, SCENE 3. Evening

*To open*:  Late dusk with light gradually fading as scene progresses; lighting from house, practicals on with covering spots

| *Cue* 9 | **Michael** pauses and listens | (Page 58) |
| | *Flash of swivelling car headlights; headlights switched off* | |

# EFFECTS PLOT

## ACT I

## ACT II

| | | |
|---|---|---|
| *Cue* 12 | **Ralph**: "It could well happen suddenly, yes."<br>*Printer stops* | (Page 43) |
| *Cue* 13 | **Ralph**: " ... or I might even beat it ..."<br>*Car approaching, then stopping* | (Page 49) |
| *Cue* 14 | **Michael**: "In your study?"<br>*Car door opening then slamming closed* | (Page 49) |
| *Cue* 15 | **Anna**: "Bad news?"<br>*Swimming/water noises from swimming pool* | (Page 53) |
| *Cue* 16 | **Ralph**: "That's got me out."<br>*Sounds of someone leaving a swimming pool* | (Page 54) |
| *Cue* 17 | **Michael** begins to move to the hosue<br>*Car approaching; stopping; engine switched off; car<br>    door closing* | (Page 58) |